KiDS'
Guide to
Bible
Animals

JANE LANDRETH

BARBOUR
PUBLISHING

D1511438

ISBN 978-1-60260-951-8

Published by Barbour Publishing, Inc., P.O. Box 719, Uhrichsville, Ohio 44683 www.barbourbooks.com

Our mission is to publish and distribute inspirational products offering exceptional value and biblical encouragement to the masses.

Member of the
Evangelical Christian
Publishers Association

Printed in the United States of America.

RR Donnelley, Willard, OH 44890; April 2011; D10002718

CONTENTS

CONTENTS

INTRODUCTION

Wouldn't it have been exciting to watch God create all the living creatures on the fifth and sixth days of creation week?

How much fun God must have had creating all those animals! He made creatures with eight legs, six legs, four legs, two legs, and no legs. He even made some with hundreds of legs! He shaped animals with arms and no arms. God fashioned animals with long necks, short necks, and even no necks. He formed animals with one hump, two humps, and no humps. He created fat animals and skinny animals, long and short animals.

God made some animals to live on the ground and some to live in trees. He made some to live in the cliffs of the mountains and some to burrow under the ground. He produced some to swim in the deepest oceans and some to live near the seashore. God created some animals to soar with the air currents, while others have to work hard to even get off the ground.

Wow! What an awesome God!

Our God is so powerful and mighty that He created dinosaurs that stretched up to forty feet tall, and yet He is so gentle that He made delicate insects smaller than a pinhead. And He created all the animals in between.

And when God had created all the living creatures on land and in the water, He looked over His creation and said, "It is good!"

I had fun researching these animals for you. I learned a lot of new things—just as you will as you read about these animals. I've used easy-to-read names for the different types of animals:

AMPHIBIANS: These cold-blooded creatures have backbones and skeletons and live part of their lives in water and part on land.

BIRDS: These warm-blooded animals have feathers and wings, though not all of them can fly. They come in many sizes, colors, shapes, and behavior patterns.

MAMMALS: These warm-blooded animals live on the land, in the sea, in the air, or underground. They have fur or hair, and most of them give birth to live young rather than laying eggs.

ANNELIDS: These are segmented worms—just like the common earthworms that burrow in the soil.

FISH: These water creatures, which come in a wide variety of shapes and colors, have fins and use gills to breathe. Most of them have scales on their bodies.

MOLLUSKS: Most of these animals live in water, and many of them have hard shells. Snails and shellfish are mollusks. So are slugs, octopuses, and squids.

ARACHNIDS: Creepy, crawly animals with an external skeleton and eight legs, such as spiders and scorpions.

INSECTS: These hard-bodied animals have six legs and three-part bodies (the head, the thorax, and the abdomen). Some of them can fly, and some of them can't.

REPTILES: These creatures are cold-blooded and have bodies covered with scales. Snakes, lizards, and turtles are reptiles.

INTRODUCTION

I have mentioned the Mosaic Law several times in this book. Many centuries ago, God gave His people, the Israelites, these laws through Moses. God was instructing His people in how to live, eat, and worship. God allowed the Israelites to eat many of the animals listed in this book, but He told them not to eat others.

I hope that you enjoy reading and learning about all the animals written about in the following pages. Of course, we know that God created more animals than the one hundred listed here, but I included only the ones named in the Bible.

So go ahead and enjoy reading about the animals. As you read, think about the fun God must have had as He created each one.

Sincerely,
Jane Landreth

Thank you to my husband, Jack,
who encouraged me as I researched and wrote;
he even helped gather some of the information for me.

Type of animal:

Insect

Find it in the Bible:

Proverbs 6:6

ANT

THAT'S A BIG FAMILY!

The ant is a social insect that lives in a large family called a "colony." An ant colony can be very big—sometimes numbering in the millions of individual ants. The colony is divided into a social order of queens, males, and workers. The survival of the ant colony depends on each member doing what it was designed to do.

The queen ants are the largest in the colony. The queen's job is to lay eggs, which ensures the colony's survival and growth. After a queen mates for the first time, she hunts for a crack in the soil and digs a little chamber, where she seals herself inside and lays her first batch of eggs. She guards them until they hatch. After her single mating, the queen can lay fertilized eggs for several years without mating again.

The worker ants are females that never reproduce. Their jobs are to gather food, to care for the young ants, to work on nests, to protect the colony, and to perform other duties. The male ants mate with queens and then die. Soldier ants find new places for nests.

Ants do not have ears, but they "hear" vibrations through sensory organs. They talk to one another by touching antennas. When two ants meet, they stroke antennas to feel and smell what the other ant has to say. As the feelers brush, the ants swap scents that contain messages about food, eggs, danger, and other information that has to do with the colony. The touching of antennas also helps identify strangers who may be trying to get into the nest to cause damage.

There are many species of ants, and they all behave differently from one another. Some ants eat meat, while others eat mostly vegetation. Some ants capture and hold other insects like aphids and other ants as slaves. Some conduct war on other ant colonies. Some ant colonies even have a regular army of soldiers to protect them from danger.

The larger, winged "queen ant" lays eggs deep in the ground while other "worker ants" gather food or guard the colony.

For most ants, colony life centers around the nest. The nest is a community constructed underground, in ground-level mounds, or even in trees. The nest is a maze of tunnels. It is a very busy place that can become very crowded with industrious ants working to keep the colony functioning.

Some ants live in constructed complex nests that resemble miniature cities. These ants build homes that are several stories high—sometimes five hundred times higher than the builder ant is tall. Some nests may reach twenty feet below ground, while others may be five feet tall.

WOW! WHAT A BIG HOUSE!

The nests have chambers for laying eggs, a nursery, places for food storage, resting places for workers, and rooms for mating. The many rooms, corridors, and vaulted rooms can cover an area as large as a tennis court.

The ant is mentioned twice in the Bible, both times in the book of Proverbs, which praises the ant for its wisdom in providing for itself. The ant is not lazy and does not put off the work it must do to survive. In Proverbs 30:24–25, the ant is said to have much wisdom and ability even though it is very small. This passage holds up the ant as a worthy example to us humans.

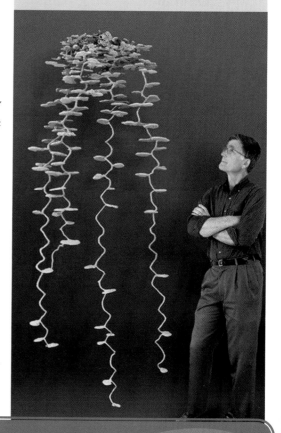

What on earth is that? Actually, it's under the earth. A man studies a plaster cast made from an underground ant colony.

DID YOU KNOW. . .

- Some ants can lift and carry up to fifty times their own weight.
- Queen ants can live up to twenty years.
- The dirt that piles up around the colony entryway is called an "anthill."
- One ant colony in Japan has forty-five thousand connected nests containing 300 million individuals, including more than 1 million queens.

ANTELOPE

Type of animal:	Find it in the Bible:
Mammal	Deuteronomy 14:5–6 NIV

WHAT'S A CUD CHEWER?

The antelope is a hoofed animal from the same group as cattle. There are about ninety different species of antelope.

The antelope has long, bony horns that stretch backward from its head. The antelope's horns do not branch out from the central horn. Unlike most other hoofed animals, the antelope never sheds its horns. The antelope has a dense coat of brown fur with black markings and a tuft of black hair under its neck.

The antelope has keen senses of sight, smell, and hearing. Its eyes are located on the side of its head, giving it broad vision. Using its senses of smell and hearing, it can sense danger when its enemies are near.

The antelope uses its powerful legs to make spectacular leaps as high as eight feet. When the antelope leaps and kicks, the enemy is confused. Some antelope can run as fast as 60 miles per hour, making it easy for them to outrun their enemies.

The antelope can use its horns as a weapon to defend itself against a predator, but more often it uses them in competitive clashes with another antelope over a potential mate.

A CUD IS A FOOD BALL THAT IS KEPT IN A SPECIAL PART OF THE STOMACH AND BROUGHT UP LATER TO CHEW AND DIGEST.

In the Mosaic Law, antelope are listed as clean animals, so the Israelites could hunt and eat them. The Israelites were allowed to eat animals that had a split hoof and chewed the cud, which means they swallow the food and bring it back up to chew later. The antelope ate the leaves, grass, fruit, mushrooms, and twigs that grew in the grasslands of the Bible lands.

DID YOU KNOW. . .

- A group of antelope is called a "herd."

- Some antelope make warning noises that sound like a barking dog.

- The smallest antelope is about ten inches tall, and the largest is about six feet tall.

APE

YOU, EVOLVED FROM AN APE?

Type of animal:
Mammal
Find it in the Bible:
1 Kings 10:22

An ape is a large, long-haired primate with no tail. There are several kinds of apes, including gorillas, chimpanzees, orangutans, and others. Primates are a group of animals that includes lemurs, monkeys, and apes. Primates are known for their forward-facing eyes and flexible arms, legs, and fingers. Primates also have hands with five fingers, each of which has fingernails.

The ape's long, strong arms and short, weaker legs make it a great climber. Most apes have the ability to walk on two legs for short distances. Apes use their thumbs and toes for grasping objects. They also use their hands for gathering food or nesting materials and, in some cases, for using simple tools.

Most apes are intelligent animals that can learn easily. Some apes have even learned to use sign language to communicate with humans. The ape has a good memory and can perform tasks it has been taught in the past. It can also express humanlike emotions, such as happiness, fear, anxiety, and boredom.

Apes live in small family groups called "troops." The troops stay in one place until the apes have eaten most of the food, then move on to a new spot. Some male apes groan and roar to keep other males away from his family. The roar can be heard a half mile away. When courting, some male gorillas try to impress the females with a chest-beating display. The male gorilla makes a *pok-pok-pok* sound by cupping his hands together.

Apes are mentioned only twice in the Old Testament. They were not native to the Holy Land, but the Israelites were familiar with them. Some types, especially chimpanzees, were kept as pets. They were among the gifts that the ships of Hiram brought Solomon (see 1 Kings 10:22).

DID YOU KNOW. . .

- The smallest ape is the gibbon, and the largest is the gorilla.

- Some apes can live up to sixty years.

- Humans and apes are ticklish in the same body areas.

BABOON

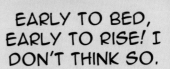

Type of animal:	Find it in the Bible:
Mammal	1 Kings 10:22 NIV

EARLY TO BED, EARLY TO RISE! I DON'T THINK SO.

DID YOU KNOW. . .

- Baboons have strong legs for walking long distances.

- The baboon has a bent tail that gives it a "sitting pad."

- Baboons can survive for long periods without finding water by licking the night dew from their fur.

Baboons are known for their bright red, hairless, built-in "sitting pads"!

The baboon, a large type of monkey, has a doglike muzzle, close-set eyes, powerful jaws, thick fur, a short tail, and rough spots on its overhanging buttocks. The buttocks are hairless pads of skin that provide for the sitting comfort of the baboon. And they are bright red!

The baboon is intelligent and crafty, and it interacts well with people. A group of baboons, which is called a "troop" or "congress," can be agricultural pests that destroy crops.

The baboon sleeps, travels, feeds, and socializes in its troop. There is usually one male among the family group, which may be as large as one hundred individuals. Baboons are omnivores, meaning they eat nearly everything. Sometimes the troop travels five or six miles a day looking for the berries, seedpods, blossoms, leaves, roots, and bark to eat. They also eat insects, fish, birds, and small mammals.

Baboons spend a lot of their time grooming and cleaning themselves and other baboons. When they wake up and come down from their sleeping perch, they begin grooming. Then they spend their day eating and napping. In the evening, they groom themselves and others again to get rid of the parasites they pick up during the day. They are usually in their sleeping perch by about six o'clock in the evening.

The baboon is mentioned only twice in the Bible. First Kings 10:22 and 2 Chronicles 9:21 tell us that once every three years a fleet of trading ships came to Israel and brought baboons, among other things, to King Solomon.

BADGER

HOW DOES THE BADGER KEEP ITS CLAWS SO SHARP?

Type of animal:
Mammal

Find it in the Bible:
Exodus 25:5 KJV

The badger is a short-legged, stocky carnivore with black and white stripes running down its face and over its head. Its body is more or less flattened, giving it the perfect shape for moving through the tunnels of its underground home. It has claws on its front legs, which it keeps sharp by scratching on trees.

The badger has a strong sense of smell and searches for food constantly by sniffing the ground. It catches most of its food—earthworms, mice, moles, and gophers—by digging with amazing speed. With its powerful front legs and claws, the badger can tunnel very quickly through soil to catch burrowing prey. At other times the badger captures prey by chasing it into burrows and then digging it out.

The badger does not hibernate during the winter but spends much of its time sleeping. When it becomes hungry, it searches for hibernating animals, digs them up, and eats them. Then when it is finished eating, the badger returns to its burrow for another time of sleeping.

A badger fiercely protects itself and its young. It is capable of fighting off much larger animals such as wolves, coyotes, and even bears.

Badger skins were used in making a tent or curtain for use in the tabernacle. Some sandals in biblical times were also made of badger skins (Ezekiel 16:10 KJV).

DID YOU KNOW...

- Badgers live underground in a system of burrows called "setts."
- American badgers grow to almost three feet long (head to tail) and to around twenty-five pounds.
- The badger can run or gallop for short distances at 15 to 19 miles per hour.
- The badger can eat as many as two hundred earthworms a day.

Type of animal:

Mammal

Find it in the Bible:

Leviticus 11:19

"BLIND AS A BAT"? HA!

BAT

The bat is the only mammal with the ability to fly. A bat's wings are made of thin skin stretched tightly between its legs, tail, arms, and fingers. These help some bats fly up to ten thousand feet above the ground and reach speeds of up to 60 miles per hour.

There are about eleven hundred species of bats living in the world today. Their size and appearance, what they eat, and how they behave depends on the kind of bat. Most bats eat insects, but many of them eat fruit and vegetables. Depending on the species, a bat's diet can include fruit, leaves, cacti, insects, small reptiles, or even other bats.

Many people think a bat cannot see at all. In truth, most bats can see well in dim light, but they use their sense of hearing to help them find food and navigate in the dark. The bat's big ears help it trap sounds. It finds bugs to eat by listening for their footsteps or wing beats.

Most bats sleep during the day in a cave or hollow tree, which is called a "roost." Their hooked claws on their wings and toes help them hang upside down or climb a wall or tree trunk. Like most other animals, a bat needs to drink water to survive. It slurps up water as it flies low over a stream. But if it flies too low—splash—it may go for a swim! No worry—it uses its wings to paddle through the water.

BATS CAN SWIM!

The bat is not dangerous to people, though some carry diseases that are harmful to people. Contrary to what many people think, the common vampire bat does not suck blood but laps it up after the razor-sharp teeth slices its food.

Bats are commonly seen in and around the dark caves of the Middle East. They are among the animals listed in the Mosaic Law as unclean.

DID YOU KNOW...

● The world's smallest bat, the Kiti's hognose bat, measures a little over one inch long and weighs less than one-tenth of an ounce.

● The world's largest bat, the flying fox, has a wingspread of up to four feet.

● Bats can catch as many as twelve hundred flying insects in one night.

BEAR

WOW!
WHAT A HUGE
BEAR!

Type of animal:
Mammal
Find it in the Bible:
2 Kings 2:24

The bear is a large, heavy animal with long, thick, shaggy hair. It has stocky legs, a long snout, paws with five claws, and a short tail. The head is large with rounded ears.

One of the most common species, the brown bear, has a shoulder hump on its back. The shoulder has superstrong muscles that help the bear roll over huge rocks and logs as it searches for food. The hump muscles and claws give the bear a powerful digging ability that lets it feast on roots, bulbs, and rodents. They also help in climbing trees and tearing apart the prey it catches.

The bear has an excellent sense of smell that helps it find food. It will eat almost anything. When it is really hungry, it may take a lamb or goat from the flock in the field.

Most bears can stand and walk on the soles of their feet, just like humans, at least for short distances. They distribute their weight toward the hind feet, which makes them look awkward when they walk. They can stand on their hind legs and sit up straight with remarkable balance. Despite their heavy build and awkward gait, most bears can run very fast. The strong muscles, powerful legs, and long claws also make the bear an excellent climber and swimmer.

Except when it is courting, the bear is typically a solitary animal. A large male will chase the younger males away from a female. Equally matched males will fight for a mate. Some bears wear scars on their heads and necks from past battles. Males may follow their

Even though bears are four-legged animals, they can stand up on their hind legs like humans.

mates around, guarding against rivals.

The bear is generally active during the day and sleeps at night. A cave or burrow in the side of a cliff is used for its den.

Before cold weather sets in, most bears forage for large amounts of food to get them ready for a long period of sleep during the winter. Some bears do not sleep all winter but come out of hibernation during warmer days to eat.

Bears were quite common in the hilly and wooded parts of Israel. The bear of the Bible has been identified, with little doubt, as the Syrian brown bear. This bear grows to as tall as six feet and weighs as much as five hundred pounds. In biblical times, the bear was a threat to vineyards and to herds of sheep and goats.

During the summer months, these bears kept to the snowy parts of Lebanon, but in the winter they traveled to villages and gardens. This bear is a large meat-eating mammal that does not hibernate because its food source lasts all year.

Shepherds guard their flocks from all dangers—including hungry bears!

DAVID AND THE BEAR

When David, the future king of Israel, was a young boy, he watched his father's sheep in the fields. He would sing to them, pour oil on their wounds, and protect them. He carried a big stick that helped fight off any animal that threatened the flock.

One day when David was watching the sheep, a bear came after one of them and started to carry it off. David went after it with his stick and beat it until it let go of the sheep.

Later, as David pleaded with King Saul to allow him to fight the giant Philistine warrior named Goliath, he told Saul how he fought off the bear that tried to steal his sheep. "I'm not afraid to fight this giant," he told the king. "I will fight for the Lord."

See 1 Samuel 17:32–37

A BIBLICAL BEAR ATTACK

Those forty-two youths who made fun of the prophet Elisha saw something like this coming for them!

One day, the Old Testament prophet Elisha was walking along the road toward Bethel. Suddenly some young men came out of town and began making fun of him. "Go on up! You don't even have any hair on your head!" they yelled.

Elisha turned and looked at the young men. Then he called a curse on them in the name of the Lord. Two bears came out of the woods and mauled forty-two of the young fellows. Elisha just continued walking down the road.

OTHER BIBLE VERSES THAT MENTION BEARS ARE 2 SAMUEL 17:8; PROVERBS 17:12; AND ISAIAH 11:7.

See 2 Kings 2:23–25

DID YOU KNOW. . .

- At over eight feet tall and up to fifteen hundred pounds, the polar bear is considered the largest bear in the world.
- Some bears can run as fast as 40 miles per hour.
- When a bear cub is born, it is about the size of a squirrel.
- The bear has good vision and sees in color, similar to humans.
- Bears are believed to have the best sense of smell of any animal on earth.

Type of animal:
Insect

Find it in the Bible:
Judges 14:8

BEE

THE QUEEN BEE MUST BE REALLY TIRED AFTER ALL THAT WORK!

Bees are social insects that live in structures called "hives." They are closely related to wasps and ants. They are important to humans because they provide sweet honey to eat and because they help pollinate the plants that supply us with fruits, grains, and vegetables.

The bee's body is bulky, so it needs wings large enough to keep it in the air but small enough to allow it to enter the hive. Its four wings hook together for flight. When it is not flying, the wings release and overlap, allowing it to enter a small area.

The bee lives in a colony that consists of as many as fifty thousand individuals. The colony includes the queen, the drones, and the workers. Each member has its own special job to do to meet the needs of the whole colony.

The queen bee is the mother of the drones, the workers, and the future queens. Her body is longer than the other bees, and she has a larger abdomen. Her jaws contain sharp cutting teeth. The queen bee is equipped with a curved, smooth stinger she can use repeatedly with no danger to her life. Unlike the worker bees, she has no pollen baskets on her legs or beeswax glands on her abdomen. Her job is to lay up to a thousand eggs a day in the honeycomb cells.

The worker bees perform several jobs. They are females who build and maintain the nests, using wax secreted from glands in their abdomens. They feed and care for the larvae produced from the eggs. They also gather nectar and pollen. They have pollen baskets on their legs and long tongues they use to suck up the nectar from flowers. They bring the nectar back to the colony, where it is converted to honey and placed in hexagonal cells.

The worker bee sometimes travels far to find pollen and nectar. She averages five trips each day. When a worker bee finds a source of nectar, she performs a "bee dance." This tells the other worker bees where the source of food is located. And off they go!

Worker bees hard at work making honey for their colony.

BEE

Another job of the worker bees is to protect the nests. Their only defense is to sting their enemies. Once they sting their victim they die, because the stinger remains in the victim, leaving a fatal wound in the bee's abdomen.

The hive's drones are stingless, defenseless males whose only function is to mate with the queen bee before they die.

Bees and honey are mentioned several times in the Bible. Bees abounded in Palestine, and their honey was a common food among the people.

THE OLD TESTAMENT TELLS ABOUT GOD LEADING THE ISRAELITES INTO A LAND "FLOWING WITH MILK AND HONEY."

SAMSON FINDS HONEY

One day Samson was visiting the vineyards with his parents. All of a sudden a roaring lion came after them. God gave Samson special powers, which he used to tear apart the lion with his bare hands.

Later, as Samson was traveling the same road, he noticed honeybees swarming around the lion's carcass. He reached inside and dug the honey out with his hands. He ate some of it as he walked down the road. When he saw his parents, he gave them some and they ate of it. He did not tell them that he had taken the honey from the lion's carcass.

Samson gave a feast, which was a custom for the bridegroom. He made up a riddle about the lion and the honey for the men at the feast to solve

You can read the whole story in Judges 14.

A beekeeper at work harvesting honey from one of his hives.

READ THE RIDDLE AND THE SOLUTION IN JUDGES 14:14-18.

JONATHAN EATS HONEY

The Israelites were fighting the Philistines. After winning the battle, Jonathan—the son of King Saul—and the army entered the woods and saw honey dripping out of a honeycomb. None of the soldiers ate any honey. They were afraid because Saul had made them take an oath not to eat any food before evening. If they did, they would be cursed.

Jonathan had not heard his father put the army under the oath. He had a long stick in his hand. He reached out and dipped the end of it into the honeycomb and put the honey into his mouth. It made him feel better. He told the men, "Look how much better I feel because I have eaten the honey. You would have felt better if you had eaten today."

You can read the whole story in 1 Samuel 14.

JOHN THE BAPTIST AND HONEY

John the Baptist spent time in the wilderness preparing to preach to the people about Jesus. During his time there, he ate locusts and wild honey.

See Matthew 3:1–4

DID YOU KNOW. . .

- The bee is the only insect that makes food you can eat.

- Bees sometimes travel as far as a mile to find pollen and nectar.

- When a bee flies, the wings move in a figure-eight pattern, allowing it to fly in any direction.

- The bee cleans its antenna with a piece of tissue on its front legs.

- Beeswax is used to make candles.

BEETLE

THOSE ARE SOME WEIRD-LOOKING INSECTS!

Type of animal:
Insect

Find it in the Bible:
Leviticus 11:22 KJV

Beetles make up the largest family of insects. There are hundreds of thousands of known species of beetles. Some are barely visible to human eyes, but some are as big as an adult human's hand. Beetles are mostly black or brown, but some are bright colors and patterns. They live in all types of environments. Some are even found in freshwater.

An adult beetle has an extra tough body and strong legs, but its most important feature is its hardened forewings that fit over its hind wings. When a beetle flies, the forewings open, but the hind wings are the ones that beat. The beetle has flattened legs with protective spines and silky hairlike strands. The hooked feet give the beetle a grip to hold objects. Large pincherlike structures on the front of the beetle move horizontally to grasp, crush, or cut food. The beetle also uses them to protect itself from enemies.

Beetles defend themselves in several ways. Some beetles use camouflage, hiding among surroundings that are colored like themselves. Some beetles mimic other insects that their enemies leave alone. Other beetles send out toxic substances that can poison predators. Still other beetles defend themselves with horns and spines.

According to the Mosaic Law, beetles are a clean animal and can be eaten.

DID YOU KNOW. . .

- The beetle uses its antennae to smell and feel its surroundings.
- There are more species of beetles than of any other animal on earth.
- The whirligig beetle, which spends much of its time on the surface of the water, has eyes that split so that it can see below and above the waterline.
- The Australian tiger beetle can run almost 6 miles per hour.

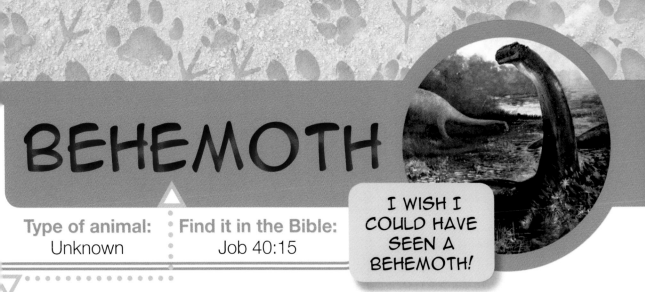

BEHEMOTH

Type of animal:
Unknown

Find it in the Bible:
Job 40:15

I WISH I COULD HAVE SEEN A BEHEMOTH!

The behemoth is a mysterious creature described in the book of Job. It is mysterious because no animal currently living on earth fits its description. Here are the biblical facts about this creature:

- **The behemoth eats grass like an ox (Job 40:15).**
- **Its strength is in its hips and in the muscles of its belly (40:16).**
- **It moves its tail like a cedar (40:17).**
- **Its bones are like beams of bronze, and its ribs are like bars of iron (40:18).**
- **It is first among the works of God (40:19).**
- **It lies under the lotus tree and hides among the reeds in the marsh (40:21).**
- **It spends time in the water (40:23).**

Bible scholars have debated for centuries exactly what the behemoth was. Was it an elephant? A hippopotamus? Or, perhaps, a dinosaur?

The elephant eats grass, but its strength is in its neck, head, and tusks, not in the "belly"—which happens to be the weakest part of the animal. Also, the elephant retreats to the forest in the hottest part of the day, not in the marshy areas. It also has a large trunk but a very short tail.

The hippopotamus also eats grass, but its tail is only twenty inches long and very thin—not at all like a cedar. It spends much time in the deep water because its skin will dry out if it spends much time lying under the trees in the marshland.

So could the behemoth have been a dinosaur? No other creature, living or extinct, fits the description in Job 40 better. Many dinosaurs had huge tails like a cedar tree. And it's safe to say that their bones were like beams of bronze and their limbs were like bars of iron.

Could the behemoth mentioned in the Bible have been what is now called a hippopotamus?

DID YOU KNOW. . .

● The book of Job gives some amazing details about the behemoth, so we know that it is not a mythical creature.

● Many fossils have been found to prove dinosaurs were once on the earth.

● The brachiosaurus was one of the largest animals (more then forty tons, eighty feet long, and forty feet tall) ever to walk on the earth.

● People use the word *behemoth* today to describe something of great size or power.

Some biblical experts believe the behemoth was just a mythical creature. Others believe the animal lived on the earth before God created man. But in the book of Job, God talked to Job about the animals He made along with man (Job 40:15). God asked Job to "look at the behemoth" as though the animal was there for Job to see at that very moment.

We can't know for sure what kind of animal the behemoth was. It is a mysterious beast that was apparently very large and powerful—and obviously one the people of Job's day were familiar with.

BITTERN

Type of animal:
Bird

Find it in the Bible:
Isaiah 34:11 KJV

THIS BIRD MUST BE HIDING!

The bittern is a bird from the heron family. It lives in marshy areas, where it uses its long bill to stab the frogs, small fish, snakes, and bugs it eats. Unlike most of the herons, it has a short neck, which it does not stretch out during flight.

When predators pursue the bittern, it stands very still with its beak pointing straight up and its neck vertical, which helps camouflage it. The bittern's yellow and brown markings and its striped neckband help it blend into the marsh grass. It may even wobble slowly to imitate the movement of the marsh reeds. The arrangement of the bird's eyes lets it see all around its surroundings and allows it to change positions so its chest always faces predators. The back of the bittern is not as well camouflaged.

The bittern relies more on camouflage to defend itself than on its flight, which is sluggish. It is not completely defenseless, for it has a sharp bill and claws. It can also puff up its body feathers to make it appear bigger to its enemies.

The bittern is most active at dawn and dusk. Its booming cry, "Oog-ka-chuk," which sounds like a deep foghorn, can be heard each night.

OTHER BIBLE TRANSLATIONS CALL THIS BIRD "BUSTARD" OR "OWL."

The King James Version of the Bible describes the land where the bittern lives as being marshy or swampy. It also describes the song of the bittern in Zephaniah 2:14.

DID YOU KNOW. . .

- The bittern can stand still for many hours if predators are lurking around.

- The bittern is very difficult to find among the reed beds of the marshland.

- The mating call of the bittern can be heard from up to two miles away.

CAMEL

CAMEL HAIR CLOTHING WOULD BE SCRATCHY!

Type of animal:

Mammal

Find it in the Bible:

Job 1:3

The camel is a large, humpbacked animal that has been important to people for thousands of years. There are two types of camel—the dromedary, which has one hump on its back, and the Bactrian, which has two humps. The camel has a long neck, and its eyes, ears, and nostrils are set high upon its head so it can spot threats from far away. To protect against the blowing sand in the desert, it kneels down, presses its ears flat, shuts its eyes and nostrils, and waits out the storm.

The camel's ears are small and lined with fur to filter out sand and dust. Its eyes are large and protected by a double row of long, curly lashes that also help keep out dust and sand. Its thick, bushy eyebrows help shield its eyes from the desert sun.

THAT HUMP IS NOT A WATER TANK!

Contrary to what many people think, the camel does not store water in its hump. Instead, it stores fat reserves in its hump, which it uses when food is scarce. When a camel goes without food or water, it lives off the fat reserve. When it does find water, it can drink as much as twenty gallons in ten minutes.

The camel is a cud-chewing animal. It gulps down its food without chewing it first. Later it regurgitates the undigested food and chews it in cud form. The camel eats thorny plants, leaves, twigs, and dried grasses, including some other animals will not eat.

A camel has two hoofed toes on each foot. It also has broad, flat, leathery pads on its feet that spread wide apart when it walks.

Camels are still important animals in some parts of the world, especially where there isn't much water to drink.

This helps prevent the camel's feet from sinking into the sand. When walking, a camel moves both feet on one side of its body, then both feet on the other. The gait is like a rolling boat, which explains the camel's nickname, "Ship of the Desert."

The dromedary camel was common among the nations of Palestine in biblical times. It was the primary mode of transportation for goods and people traveling across the dry, hot terrain. It could carry about four hundred pounds in addition to its rider.

The Bible mentions the camel about fifty times. It was of great importance in the lives of the people of biblical times. In addition to using the camel for transportation, the people used its milk for food and its hide to make clothes, rugs, tents, and other necessary items. Even the camel's droppings were used for fuel for their fires.

ABRAHAM AND HIS CAMELS

Abraham and Sarah were traveling through Egypt in the time of famine. Pharaoh had given Abraham camels along with other animals. Camels were a part of Abraham's wealth.

Years later Abraham sent his servant to find a wife for his son Isaac. The servant found a young maiden at the well who gave him water and also watered his camel. She and her maidens rode camels back so she could become Isaac's bride

See Genesis 24

CAMELS AND WEALTH

Animals, including camels, were a measure of a person's wealth in biblical times. Camels were included in the wealth of Abraham, Isaac, Jacob, and other biblical patriarchs. Job had much wealth, including three thousand camels along with other animals. Later many kings acquired camels as part of their own wealth. Camels not only meant wealth, but riders on camels brought wealth—gold and incense—from Sheba to the Lord.

In biblical times, owning large numbers of these animals—whether they were smiling or not—meant you were a very wealthy person.

JESUS TAUGHT USING THE CAMEL

Jesus taught that it was easier for a camel to go through the eye of a needle than for a rich man to enter heaven. Some scholars believe this was a traditional description of a camel kneeling down to creep under the low gate in the Jerusalem wall. If that is true, Jesus' words meant that if a rich man will rid himself of pride and humble himself (kneel), he can get into heaven (see Luke 18:25).

Jesus also described hypocrites as people who were very careful to strain out a gnat from a cup of drink but who swallowed a camel without notice. In other words, they gave a tithe of a small herb but omitted doing the important things.

See Matthew 23:24

DID YOU KNOW. . .

● The adult camel is about seven feet tall at the hump and weighs around fifteen hundred pounds.

● A camel can survive the scorching hot summers and harsh, severe winters in the desert.

● A young camel can walk one hundred miles in a day.

● Even though the camel spits when it is upset, it is considered a good-tempered, patient, and intelligent animal.

OTHER BIBLE VERSES THAT MENTION CAMELS ARE 1 SAMUEL 30:17; JEREMIAH 2:23; AND MARK 1:6.

CATERPILLAR

Type of animal:
Insect

Find it in the Bible:
Psalm 78:46 KJV

The caterpillar is the larva form of the butterfly and moth. It has a soft body that grows rapidly. It has a hard head and a strong jawbone, which it uses for chewing leaves and other vegetation. Behind the jawbone is a silk-spinning organ. The tubular body of the caterpillar has segments with many legs.

The caterpillar's body has about four thousand muscles in it. The muscles in the rear segments move the caterpillar forward.

Even though the caterpillar has six tiny eyelets on each side of the head, it does not have good vision. It judges the distances of objects by moving the head from side to side.

The caterpillar breathes through small openings along the thorax and abdominal segments. A few caterpillars are aquatic and have gills that allow them to breathe underwater.

Many animals feed on caterpillars. For defense against enemies, some caterpillars appear to look poisonous. Some actually are poisonous and shoot out acid. Some caterpillars are colored in such a way that they can hide among the plants on which they feed. Some make a silk line and drop onto the ground when disturbed. Most caterpillars have bristles on their bodies—long, fine, hairlike strands with detachable tips—that irritate the skin of those who touch them.

Destructive is how the Bible describes the caterpillar. It even caused a famine by eating the farmers' crops.

DID YOU KNOW. . .

- The caterpillar is called an "eating machine" because it eats leaves ravenously.

- Most caterpillars shed their skin four or five times as they grow to be an adult.

- The art of raising caterpillars to make silk is called "sericulture."

OTHER BIBLE VERSES WHERE CATERPILLARS (SPELLED "CATERPILLER" IN THE KING JAMES VERSION OF THE BIBLE) ARE MENTIONED ARE 1 KINGS 8:37; 2 CHRONICLES 6:28; AND ISAIAH 33:4.

CATTLE

Type of animal:
Mammal
Find it in the Bible:
Exodus 9:3

> DOES A BULL GET MAD WHEN HE SEES RED?

Cattle are very important and useful animals to humans—from biblical times until now. Most cattle are raised for milk, meat, and hides for making items. Male cattle are called "bulls" and are usually raised for meat. Female cattle are called "cows" and are usually kept for milk and to bear young. Young cattle, both male and female, are called "calves."

Cattle are often raised by allowing herds to graze on large tracts of grassland. Depending on the breed, cattle can survive and grow by grazing on hills, marshes, and semideserts. Many farmers today add commercial grains to cattle's diets.

Cattle were important in biblical times. The term *cattle* commonly referred to all domesticated animals. In populated areas, a young boy herded the cattle, but most of the time, the cattle were left alone to forage for food in nearby pastures.

From early biblical times, herds of cattle were kept to provide milk, meat, and leather from the skins. The number of cattle and sheep a person owned revealed the person's wealth.

The land of Goshen, where the Hebrews settled during the time of Joseph, was rich in cattle. Cattle were valued for sacrifices, for food, and as work animals. They were

> READ HOW BULLOCKS WERE SACRIFICED UNDER THE MOSAIC LAW IN EXODUS 29 AND LEVITICUS 1:5 AND 4:4.

For many centuries, people have allowed cattle to grow and gain weight by grazing on grass in pastures

divided into clean and unclean classifications and were covered by the law of the Sabbath. Animals, as well as their owners, were to rest on the Sabbath.

The Jews used bullocks (bulls) for sacrifices of burnt offerings to God. They had to be flawless and offered according to the Mosaic Law.

JACOB SENDS A GIFT

After Jacob had caused much trouble for his brother and family, he moved away from home. Many years later, God told Jacob and his family to go back home. Jacob sent his helpers to tell his brother Esau that he was coming home. The helpers came back and reported, "Esau is coming to meet you. He has four hundred men with him!"

Jacob was afraid. He had run away from home because he had stolen from Esau. Jacob prayed and asked God to keep him safe from his brother. Then he selected gifts to send to Esau—goats, sheep, camels, donkeys, and cattle.

Jacob and his family walked far behind the animals. When Jacob saw Esau, he bowed low over and over to show that he was sorry for the wrong things he had done. Suddenly Esau ran to him and hugged him. Jacob was forgiven.

You can read the whole story in Genesis 32–33.

ELIJAH SACRIFICES A BULL

The Old Testament prophet Elijah went to King Ahab and said, "You make the people pray to idols instead of God. Bring your people to Mount Carmel. I will show them the real God."

When Ahab and the people got to the mountain, Elijah told them to build an altar. They were to place a bull on the altar and call for their gods to burn it. Ahab and the people called and called to their gods, but nothing happened.

Elijah built his altar and laid his bull on it. Then he said to Ahab's men, "Pour water over my altar." Then Elijah prayed, "Lord, show everyone that You are the real God."

God sent fire and burned everything, even the water. The people believed and worshiped God.

You can read the whole story in 1 Kings 18:16–39.

THE PRODIGAL SON

A fatted calf is a stall-fed animal, which meant that it was forced to eat more than it wanted to eat. It was fattened and killed for special occasions, such as to feed a special guest or to make a special offering to the Lord. Jesus talked about a fatted calf in one of His parables (stories).

A father had two sons. The younger son asked the father to give him his share of the inheritance. The younger son took the money and spent it foolishly in a far-off country. Soon he had no money and was hungry. He was sorry for what he had done. He decided to go home and ask his father if he could be one of his father's servants. At least then he would have plenty to eat.

As the father looked out one day, he saw the young son coming down the road. He was filled with love for his son and ran to him and threw his arms around him. He told his servants, "Bring the fatted calf and kill it. Let's have a big dinner and celebrate my son coming home"

See Luke 15:11–31

From biblical times forward, wealthy people owned large herds of cattle.

DID YOU KNOW...

- There are more than one hundred different cattle breeds.
- Cattle are red-green color blind; therefore they are not angry when they see red.
- Some full-grown bulls weigh one thousand to four thousand pounds, and cows weigh eight hundred to twenty-four hundred pounds.
- Cattle have one stomach with four compartments for digesting grasses and vegetation.
- Cattle dung is used as a fertilizer for crops and for fuel.

OTHER VERSES USING CATTLE IN THE BIBLE ARE GENESIS 18:7; EXODUS 29:36; NUMBERS 15:8

CHAMELEON

Type of animal:
Reptile

Find it in the Bible:
Leviticus 11:30

> LOOK! THE CHAMELEON IS BROWN. NO, IT'S GREEN. NO, IT'S RED...

The chameleon is a lizard that changes color according to its surroundings. The chameleon does not just decide to change color. Its color change is a natural and unplanned reaction to something that happens to it.

The chameleon has a long, flat body with a tail that can grasp a twig just as a human hand does. When the chameleon is not using its tail, it curls it up in a spiral.

The chameleon's forefeet have little fingerlike appendages tipped with claws. The chameleon is the only lizard with a foot designed for grasping and holding.

The chameleon's bulging eyes are able to swivel in a complete circle as it constantly watches for the insects it eats. Each eyeball moves independently, allowing the chameleon to see two ways at the same time. Its keen vision can detect the smallest fly on leaves several feet away. Those same keen eyes, combined with a quick flick of the tongue, keep the chameleon well fed.

The chameleon's tongue is usually as long as its entire body. In some species, it is twice as long. It darts out quickly to capture lunch on its sticky tip. This is a most useful tool for the chameleon, a slow-moving, hard-of-hearing reptile that lives almost its entire life in trees.

The chameleon is listed as an unclean animal because it moves on the ground. In Palestine it lives in trees and bushes and hangs on to branches with its long tail.

DID YOU KNOW. . .

- The chameleon can catch its dinner in less than one second.
- Some chameleons have hornlike ridges on their heads that make them look like tiny dinosaurs.
- Chameleons vary in size from one and a half inches to three feet long.

COBRA

Type of animal:
Reptile
Find it in the Bible:
Psalm 91:13

WHY DOES THE COBRA STAND UP?

The cobra is a deadly poisonous snake with loose skin on its neck that forms a hood when the cobra is excited. The cobra rears up with its hood spread when it is provoked.

This strange creature can actually throw its poison. It knows where it will do the most harm—the eyes. The snake tilts its head back, hisses loudly, and points its fangs at the face of its victim. Suddenly, it contracts the muscles around its poison glands and lets yellow liquid fly out of its fangs in two thin jets. The poison frequently causes blindness and agonizing pain.

The cobra lives where the weather is very warm. It abides in areas around human settlements or where crops grow—both places where rodents thrive. It eats rodents, lizards, frogs, and even other snakes. Most species have poor eyesight and hunt at dusk or at night when its sight is sharper. The exception is the king cobra, which is active in the daytime and can see objects more than 330 feet away.

The cobra often lay concealed in hedges and holes in the walls of biblical cities. In the Bible, it is usually a symbol of evil. The Bible likens the poison of cobras to different negative attitudes in people, such as bitterness (see Deuteronomy 32:33). The cobra was also the snake on which the serpent charmers practiced their art.

DID YOU KNOW...

- At up to almost nineteen feet long, the king cobra is the longest venomous snake in the world.

- The cobra can throw its poison as far as nine feet.

- The cobra can live up to twenty years.

Type of animal:
Mammal
Find it in the Bible:
Leviticus 11:5

CONEY

PEW! THOSE SMELLY FEET GIVE THE CONEY TRACTION.

The coney is a small, short-eared, burrowing creature with a squat, furry body, short, slender legs, a short tail, and rodentlike incisors. The coney is not a rodent but a member of the same family as rabbits and hares.

The small hooves on its toes, along with moist padded soles, help the coney cling to steep surfaces by suction. The coney is an excellent climber that can even scale vertical cliffs. The coney's feet perspire to give it added traction.

The coney is a slow-moving animal, making it a target for predators. But the cliffs and rocks in which it lives ensure that enemies keep their distance and also protect from rain and wind. The coney stays close to home, only going out to find food.

The greatest threat to the coney is the eagle. Circling high overhead, the eagle sees the coney on the rocks. The coney's defense against eagles is its amazing eyesight, which allows it to detect movement from up to a mile away. When a coney sees an enemy, it lets out a sharp bark to warn other conies of danger.

Conies live in colonies of up to fifty animals. This is not only for protection but for warmth. The animals cuddle, sometimes lying one on top of another, to share body heat.

The coney, which lives in the hills and deserts of Palestine, is listed in the Mosaic Law as an unclean animal.

IN PROVERBS 30:26, CONIES ARE LISTED AMONG THE FOUR THINGS ON EARTH THAT ARE SMALL AND WISE.

DID YOU KNOW. . .

● The coney is sometimes called "rock badger" or "rock rabbit."

● In extreme weather, conies may lie on top of one another four layers deep to stay warm.

● In large numbers, conies can be agricultural pests.

33

CORMORANT

CORMORANTS ARE "CLOWNS" OF THE WATER.

Type of animal:
Bird

Find it in the Bible:
Leviticus 11:17

The cormorant is a medium-sized to large seabird found in many parts of the world where there are fish to catch. About forty species of cormorants are known today.

The cormorant is a superb swimmer, diver, fisher, and flyer. It has a long neck and a long, hooked beak that allows it to grasp and dig into the fish it catches. Its feet are webbed between four toes, which helps the bird to propel itself underwater. Its waterproof feathers do not trap air as do the feathers of other birds. That allows the cormorant to dive more quickly and chase prey underwater.

The cormorant can locate fish while flying high in the sky. It does not dive from the air but lands first and then dives under. The cormorant can dive as deep as thirty-three feet.

Even though the cormorant performs gracefully in the air and water, its takeoff from the water is awkward. It makes a long upwind run, flapping furiously and splashing water. It then pushes off with both feet, appearing to run across the water.

The male cormorant courts his mate by spreading his wings wide and sailing along on top of the water. He performs skillful dives, popping up and down like a cork. Often he will make a deep dive to gather rockweed, which he tosses into the air, catches, and presents to his courting mate. When she accepts, the male sits in a tree and sings "okay, okay, okay."

Cormorants are listed in the Mosaic Law as unclean, meaning they were not to be eaten.

DID YOU KNOW. . .

- Fishermen in some parts of the world sometimes call the cormorant the "submarine bird."
- After swimming, cormorants often go ashore and hold out their wings for the sun to dry them.
- People have used specially trained cormorants to catch fish.

Type of animal:

Bird

Find it in the Bible:

Isaiah 38:14 KJV

CRANE

WHO DOES THE "CRANE DANCE"?

The crane is a long-necked bird that stands about four feet tall. It has long legs, long, wide wings, and a long, pointed beak. Cranes look a lot like herons, but the two are not closely related.

There are fifteen species of cranes. Most cranes are gray with some white and black on the feathers. The sandhill crane has red skin on top of its head. The African crown crane is covered with black feathers and has a fan-shaped crest of strawlike feathers on its head.

Cranes live in well-organized groups for protection against predators. Several individual birds stand off from the group to guard against danger. Cranes use their powerful voices to communicate with other cranes when predators approach.

During certain times of the year, some cranes perform a ritual dance in which adult males, females, and young birds take part. The birds walk around each other, taking stiff-legged steps with their wings half spread. They bob their heads and bow to each other. As the dance tempo becomes faster, the cranes leap into the air. Some of them use their bills to snatch up sticks and leaves, throwing them into the air and stabbing them with their bills as they fall.

As mentioned in Jeremiah 8:7, many cranes are migratory birds that travel long distances. Most cranes mate for life and return to the same nest year after year.

SOME BIBLE TRANSLATIONS USE "SWIFT" OR "THRUSH" INSTEAD OF "CRANE."

DID YOU KNOW. . .

- The windpipe of an adult crane is five feet long and is coiled inside the breastbone.

- The loud call of the crane is similar to the sound of a trombone and can be heard as far as a mile away.

- The female crane lays two eggs, and both male and female take turns sitting on the eggs until they hatch.

CRICKET

DOES THE CRICKET PLAY A FIDDLE?

Type of animal:
Insect

Find it in the Bible:
Leviticus 11:22

A cricket is an insect related to the grasshopper and even more closely related to the katydid. It has long, jointed back legs for jumping on the ground, long antennae, and forewings that bend over its sides. It finds shelter under logs, stones, and burrows, and sometimes in buildings. It eats decaying plant material, fungi, and seedling plants. When food is scarce, the cricket will eat weakened or dead crickets.

The cricket produces a well-known song or chirp that is often heard on warm summer evenings. Only the male sings, and he does it to attract females. The cricket makes this sound by a method called "stridulation," which is by the vibration of the specially shaped forewings. On the underside of the right forewing is a vein that looks like a file. The vein is rubbed rapidly against a scraper on the upper side of the left forewing, much like the bow on a fiddle. The song helps guide the female to the male.

There are about nine hundred different species of crickets. Most of them are nocturnal, meaning they move and feed at night.

The mole cricket has powerful forelegs with claws shaped like tiny shovels. It digs burrows and moves earth. It can move a load of earth weighing as much as two pounds.

The snowy tree cricket is also called the "thermometer" cricket, because the outdoor temperature can be calculated by counting the number of times it chirps in fifteen seconds and adding thirty-nine. As the temperature warms, the tree cricket chirps faster.

According to the Mosaic Law, most flying insects are unclean and are not to be eaten. But the Bible says that crickets are permitted for food.

DID YOU KNOW...

- Crickets have powerful jaws, and some have been known to bite humans.
- A cricket hears with "ears" on the upper part of its front legs.
- In large numbers, crickets can destroy seedlings and cause great damage to farm crops.

CUCKOO

Type of animal:
Bird

Find it in the Bible:
Deuteronomy 14:15 KJV

DOESN'T THAT HAIRY CATERPILLAR TICKLE GOING DOWN?

The cuckoo (spelled "cuckow" in the King James Version of the Bible) is a medium-sized bird that ranges in size from the little bronze cuckoo, which grows to about six inches long, to the channel-billed cuckoo, which can grow to twenty-five inches long and weigh up to a pound and a half.

The cuckoo uses its slender wings and long tail for steering and as a rudder during flights—much like the rudder on an airplane.

The cuckoo gets its name from the distinctive call of the male common cuckoo. It is heard to say, "Cuck-oo, cuck-oo," combined sometimes with an angry "Kow, kow, kow." The female cuckoo doesn't make this sound.

A female cuckoo prefers to lay her eggs in another bird's nest and let the "foster parents" raise her young. When it is time to lay eggs, she finds a nest and removes the other bird's eggs with her bill then lays an egg of her own in their place. She throws the discarded eggs to the ground or eats them.

When the baby cuckoo hatches, the first thing it does is push the other eggs out of the nest. This tiny, featherless creature has a special hollow back that helps it accomplish that task. This is essential to the young cuckoo's survival, because it is much larger than other offspring and needs all the nutrition the foster parents can give it.

According to the Mosaic Law, the cuckoo is unclean and is not to be eaten. It spends its winters in Africa but migrates to parts of Europe and Asia, including the Mediterranean area, each spring to mate.

DID YOU KNOW. . .

- The cuckoo is a shy bird and is usually heard instead of seen.

- The cuckoo will eat adult insects but prefers hairy caterpillars.

- On each cuckoo's foot are two inner toes pointing forward and two outer toes pointing backward.

SOME BIBLE TRANSLATIONS CALL THE CUCKOO BIRD A "GULL."

DEER

IMAGINE CARRYING AROUND A RACK OF ANTLERS ON YOUR HEAD AS HEAVY AS A SACK OF POTATOES!

Type of animal:
Mammal
Find it in the Bible:
Psalm 42:1

The deer is an antlered animal (all males and some females, depending on the species, have antlers) with two large and two small hooves on its feet. The deer's hooves give the deer a good grip for running on hard ground.

The deer's antlers are made of dead bone and covered with a special layer of skin. During certain times of the year, the antlers are covered with a soft, fuzzy covering called "velvet." Male deer use the antlers to fight for mates—mostly shoving one another around instead of actually fighting. Deer shed their antlers each year and grow a new set.

The deer is a timid creature that can sometimes be seen near water. It is a good swimmer, which sometimes helps it escape from predators. It lives on a diet of leaves, grass, twigs, fruit, and mushrooms. A deer will spend up to twelve hours a day eating.

Deer are color blind, meaning they see everything around them in shades of gray. Their keen senses of sight, smell, and hearing alert them to movement, including that of predators.

The deer's sandy coloring sometimes makes it difficult to spot. Sometimes when a deer is

The fallow deer is known for its strange-looking antlers...kind of like a shovel!

alarmed, it will thump the ground with its front feet as if playing a drum. This warns the other deer of danger. Deer have no defense from predators other than to run from them. Wolves and cougars, along with dogs, are the deer's primary predators.

It is believed that three species of deer lived in Palestine in biblical times: the red, fallow, and roe. The red deer is the largest of the deer family and one of the most easily identifiable. It was probably the species in the list of daily provisions for Solomon's table (see 1 Kings 4:23). In the King James Bible, the hart is the male red deer, and the hind is the female.

The fallow deer has especially large, shovel-shaped antlers. It is light brown with white spots on its body. It prefers to live in herds and is valued for its meat, which is called "venison."

The roe deer is much smaller than the other two, with smaller antlers. It has a reddish body and a gray face and lives a solitary life, except during mating season.

According to Mosaic Law, the deer is considered a clean animal, which means the people of Israel could eat it. It has split hooves and chews the cud, meaning it swallows its food without chewing then brings it back up later to be chewed.

THERE'S A COOL PRAISE SONG ABOUT THE DEER PANTING!

The deer provides the Bible writers with a picture of gracefulness, swiftness, and gentleness. David wrote of the deer in many of his psalms, such as when he likens his thirsty soul longing for God to thirsty deer panting for water (Psalm 42:1). David also compares the deer to fighting men (2 Samuel 2:18 KJV).

DID YOU KNOW. . .

- A male deer is called a "buck," a female is called a "doe," and the babies are called "fawns."

- Deer tend to stay within a fairly small territory, no bigger than one square mile.

- Some deer can jump obstacles ten feet high (the height of two cars stacked on top of each other).

- In one big leap, some deer can cover the distance the length of a family van.

DOG

WOW! I DIDN'T KNOW THERE WERE SO MANY KINDS!

Type of animal:
Mammal
Find it in the Bible:
Luke 16:21

Dogs come in a variety of sizes and colors. They can be as small as a Chihuahua, which is only six to ten inches tall, and as large as the Irish wolfhound, which can grow to the height of a small pony and weigh more than 150 pounds. They come in colors ranging from white to gray to black to many shades of brown—and in a wide variation of color combinations and patterns. Their coats can be short or long, coarse or soft, straight or curly, or smooth or wool-like. It is common for most breeds to shed their coats. Dog tails can be straight, sickle-shaped, curled, or corkscrew-shaped. It is estimated that there are more than 400 million dogs living in the world today.

Domestic dogs play many important roles in people's lives. Dogs are used for hunting, for herding, for protection, for companionship, for law enforcement, and for assisting the disabled. Dogs are intelligent animals capable of learning in a number of ways, such as through reinforcement and by observation. One of the best ways for a puppy to learn is to watch an adult dog perform a task.

Even though dogs have red-green color blindness, most of them have good vision. They are able to distinguish between humans from distances of up to a mile. They are also very good at seeing moving objects.

Dogs can identify a sound's location much faster than a human can, and they can hear sounds from about four times the distance. They have highly sensitive noses, which makes them good trackers and police animals.

Wild dogs are predators and scavengers. They have powerful muscles and are strong in endurance. They use their strength and their teeth to catch and devour their prey.

Dogs are mentioned many times in the Bible, but no specific breed is identified. During biblical times, ferocious wild dogs ran in packs around fields and city streets, devouring dead bodies and other things.

Puppies are playful, curious, and energetic. They learn quickly by watching grown-up dogs.

THE RICH MAN AND LAZARUS

Dogs are called man's best friend because they really make good friends!

Jesus used dogs to teach people important truths. He told the story of the rich man and Lazarus. The rich man dressed in purple robes and fine linen. He lived an easy life, while Lazarus was a beggar who was covered with sores, which the dogs came and licked (see Luke 16:19–31).

In biblical times, calling someone a dog was a way of insulting that person. In the Old Testament, the prophet Isaiah insulted the priests of his time by saying their sacrifices were no better than breaking a dog's neck and sacrificing it. That meant they were sacrificing in the wrong way. In the New Testament, the apostle Paul warned Christians to be watchful for those who do evil and called his enemies dogs. The Jews scornfully called Gentiles "dogs."

The Bible mentions two kinds of domesticated dogs. The first is a wolflike, short-haired animal that stands guard over tents or houses and barks fiercely at strangers. These dogs ate whatever was tossed to them. At evening the dogs barked throughout the city.

The second kind of dog helped shepherds round up sheep. Dogs also served as watchdogs for herds. Job referred to the dogs as watching over his flocks. Other dogs were trained for hunting.

DID YOU KNOW. . .

- A dog's nickname is "man's best friend."
- Dogs can detect sounds from much farther distances than humans can.
- Many dog breeds have a "blaze" or "star" of white fur on their chest or underside.
- The border collie is considered one of the most intelligent dog breeds.

DONKEY

DONKEYS MAKE ME LAUGH WITH THEIR "HEE HAW, HEE HAW."

Type of animal:
Mammal

Find it in the Bible:
Luke 10:34

The donkey is a relative of the horse. It is usually gray in color and has long, pointed ears and a long tail. The tall ears pick up distant sounds and also help cool the donkey during hot weather. It is a very strong animal, which makes it ideal for doing hard work, such as pulling wagons and plows to help farmers with their crops.

The wild donkey lives in rocky places and can survive on very little water. It eats tough, spiky grass to survive in barren environments. It also grazes on herbs and even tree bark when food is scarce.

The donkey makes a good guard animal. It can look after entire herds of cattle, sheep, or goats. It defends itself with a powerful kick of its hind legs as well as by biting.

A donkey has a reputation for being stubborn. But it actually just prefers to do what is good for itself, which is not always what its human master thinks is best. This is probably because of a strong sense of self-preservation.

Donkeys were common "beasts of burden" in biblical times. They were highly valued for riding, for carrying loads, for drawing chariots or carts, and for pulling plows and doing other fieldwork. The Israelites considered donkeys unclean and unacceptable to eat.

In biblical times, donkeys were valued as pack animals. They still are today!

Knowing that animals, like people, needed time to rest, God included them when He gave the laws concerning rest on the Sabbath.

Abraham, Jacob, and many others are mentioned in the Bible as having large herds of donkeys. The animal is mentioned about 120 times in the Bible, so donkeys were obviously important animals in biblical times. The Bible says that donkeys were used for riding (Numbers 22:21), as beasts of burden (1 Samuel 16:20), and as helpers for agricultural work (Deuteronomy 22:10).

When the Israelites returned to Palestine from the Babylonian captivity, they brought with them more than six thousand donkeys, which was about six times the number of horses and camels they possessed.

Would you feel rich if you owned a bunch of these? In biblical times, people who owned lots of donkeys were considered rich.

THE TALKING DONKEY

Balaam saddled his donkey and went to a place God had told him not to go. God sent an angel to stand in the road. When the donkey saw the angel of the Lord, she turned off the road. Balaam beat the donkey to get her back on the road.

Later the angel of the Lord stood in a narrow path between two vineyards with walls on each side. When the donkey saw the angel, she crushed Balaam's foot against the wall. Balaam beat the donkey again.

Once again the angel of the Lord moved ahead and stood in a narrow place. When the donkey saw the angel, she lay down. Balaam was very angry and beat her again. Then God opened the donkey's mouth and the donkey spoke to Balaam.

SOME OTHER BIBLE VERSES THAT MENTION THE DONKEY ARE GENESIS 22:3; NUMBERS 22:28; 1 SAMUEL 9:3; AND MATTHEW 21:2.

See Numbers 22

THE GOOD SAMARITAN'S DONKEY

Jesus used the donkey in His teaching when someone asked Him, "Who is my neighbor?"

The story went like this: A man was traveling from Jerusalem to Jericho when robbers jumped him, took his clothes, beat him, and left him by the side of the road. A priest and a Levite came by the man and ignored him. But when a Samaritan came by the man and saw him, he felt sorry for him. The Samaritan bandaged the poor man's wounds and put him on his own donkey and took him to an inn.

You can read the whole story in Luke 10:25–37.

JESUS RIDES A DONKEY INTO JERUSALEM

Because of its strength and usefulness to people, the donkey became a symbol for kings in the Bible. Even Jesus rode a donkey when He entered Jerusalem.

As Jesus and His disciples approached Jerusalem, He sent two of His disciples ahead to a village to find a donkey. The disciples did what Jesus told them to do. They brought the donkey and placed their coats on it. Jesus entered Jerusalem riding on the donkey through a large crowd of people who were waiting for Him. The people spread their coats and palm branches on the road and shouted, "Hosanna to the Son of David!"

You can read this whole story in Matthew 21:1–11.

DID YOU KNOW...

- Many donkeys live to be more than twenty years old.
- Donkeys can go as long as twelve hours between meals.
- A male donkey is called a "jack" and a female is called a "jenny."
- A donkey's favorite pastime is to roll.
- Donkeys are friendly and enjoy being around people.

Type of animal:

Bird

Find it in the Bible:

Leviticus 1:14

DOVE

THE TURTLEDOVE IS A SYMBOL OF LOVE.

The dove has a small, stocky body, a short neck, and a short, slender tail. It is closely related to the pigeon.

There are more than three hundred different species of doves, and each species is colored differently. The common ground dove has chestnut-colored wing patches, a drab pink chest, and a small bill that is reddish at the base and black on the tip. The mourning dove is a slender brown bird with a white-bordered tail. The turtledove has a gray head and a body that is a beige color blushed with pink.

All species of doves fly fast on powerful wings with their tails stretched behind them. They sometimes make sudden midflight ascents, descents, and dodges. When doves take off, their wings make a sharp whistling or whining sound.

The dove forages on the ground for seeds and grain to eat. Unlike most birds, it uses its bill like a straw to suck up water.

The mating display of the male dove involves strutting up and down. The male puffs up the feathers around his throat and (in some species) raises his crest. The cooing sound he makes calms the female dove.

The female dove lays only one or two eggs at a time, but she can lay eggs several times a year. When the eggs hatch, both parents feed them special milk from pouches inside their throats called "crops."

The dove is a common and important Bible bird. It was important as a sacrifice during Old Testament times. Doves alone (or sometimes with other animals) were a sacrifice called for in Mosaic Law. Those who couldn't afford a lamb or goat as a sacrifice could use two doves for sacrifices (Leviticus 5:7–11). When Mary and Joseph brought baby Jesus to the temple, Mary brought a sacrifice of two doves (Luke 2:24).

Doves have powerful wings that help them to fly very fast and make acrobatic moves in midair!

NOAH AND THE DOVE

The first mention of the dove in the Bible was in the story of Noah and the ark. After Noah had been in the ark with the animals many days, he sent out a raven. It found no place to land. Later Noah sent out one of the doves. It came back because there was no place to land.

Noah waited seven more days. Then he let out the dove again. Noah waited and watched. Finally, the dove returned to the ark. This time it had an olive leaf in its beak.

Seven days later, Noah sent the dove out again. This time the little bird did not come back. Noah knew the waters had dried up and knew that God had kept His promise

You can read the whole story in Genesis 8:6–12.

THE DOVE AT JESUS' BAPTISM

All four Gospels in the New Testament record the appearance of a dove at Jesus' baptism. One day while John the Baptist was preaching, Jesus came to him and said, "Please baptize Me." John then led Jesus into the Jordan River and baptized Him.

As Jesus came out of the water, He saw heaven open and the Spirit descending on him like a dove. A voice from heaven said, "You are my Son, whom I love. I am well pleased with You"

See Mark 1:9–11

DID YOU KNOW. . .

- The dove is the smallest species of the pigeon family.

- The male dove can be heard in early morning singing his deep "coo, coo, coo."

- Doves are helpful to farmers, for they pick up wasted grains and weed seed.

- The white dove has become a symbol of peace.

OTHER BIBLE VERSES THAT MENTION DOVES ARE NUMBERS 6:10; PSALM 55:6; ISAIAH 38:14; AND MATTHEW 10:16

DRAGON

Type of animal:
Reptile?

Find it in the Bible:
Psalm 91:13 KJV

ARE DRAGONS ONLY IN FANTASY STORIES?

The dragon is a mythical fire-breathing animal with bat wings, sharp claws, and a barbed tail. The dragon is also described as a large dinosaur-like creature that once lived in swamps. In ancient times, coiled sea serpents were sometimes called "dragons."

What does the Bible say about dragons? It says that the dragon is a great land or sea monster, usually some type of reptile. It is powerful and deadly. Bible translations differ in what they call the dragon:

"Their wine is the poison of dragons" (Deuteronomy 32:33 KJV). Other Bible translations use the word serpents.

"Though thou hast sore broken us in the place of dragons. . ." (Psalm 44:19 KJV). Other translations used the word jackal.

"The great dragon that lieth in the midst of his rivers. . ." (Ezekiel 29:3 KJV, RSV). Other translations used the word monster.

Other Bible translations replace "dragon" with "sea monster," "whale," "snake," or "crocodile." The apostle John wrote of a mythological sea monster that symbolizes the forces of evil opposing God (see Revelation 12:3–4).

DID YOU KNOW. . .

- Lizards (some of them very large) called komodo dragons, Chinese water dragons, and bearded dragons, still exist today.

- Komodo dragons have been known to grow nearly ten feet in length.

OTHER BIBLE VERSES THAT INCLUDE THE WORD DRAGON ARE JOB 30:29 AND ISAIAH 43:20.

This is a modern-day dragon—a real one! Komodo dragons are the world's largest lizards.

EAGLE

Type of animal:
Bird
Find it in the Bible:
Isaiah 40:31

WOULD THE EAGLE BE CALLED "KING OF THE AIR"?

The eagle is a bird of prey that can be found in many parts of the world. It is powerful and majestic as it flies through the sky. Its body is small and weighs very little, allowing the eagle to soar in the air for a long period of time. It is active during the daytime rather than at night.

The eagle is an excellent hunter. It sees prey such as rabbits from as far away as two miles. It can also spot fish from several hundred feet in the air. Once the eagle has spotted its prey, it uses its strong feet with sharp talons to catch it. The powerful hooked bill tears open the flesh of the captured prey.

The nest of the American bald eagle is enormous—eight feet across and weighing as much as a ton. Eagles build their nests (which are called "eyries") in cliffs, on broad ledges, or in tall trees. They use twigs and leaves for building materials.

Though the eagle is listed in the Mosaic Law as unclean, this majestic bird has an important role in the Bible. The Old Testament writers noted the eagle's swift movements, the power of its flight, and its care for its young. In the ancient world, the eagle often was associated figuratively with God's protection and care.

Throughout history the eagle has been seen as a symbol of courage and strength. The figure of the eagle is now and has long been a favorite military emblem.

OTHER BIBLE VERSES THAT MENTION THE EAGLE ARE 2 SAMUEL 1:23; JOB 39:27; JEREMIAH 48:40 AND EZEKIEL 17:3.

DID YOU KNOW. . .

- The bald eagle can fly as fast as 60 miles per hour but can reach 100 miles per hour when it dives.
- The average adult golden eagle has a wingspan of more than seven feet.
- An eagle can swim by propelling itself through the water with its wings.

FALCON

Type of animal:
Bird

Find it in the Bible:
Deuteronomy 14:13

IS THAT BIRD ON A CRASH COURSE?

The falcon is a bird of prey with powerful feet, talons, and a heavy, hooked beak it uses to kill and tear apart its prey. It is sometimes mistaken for a hawk, but it has longer, more pointed wings than a hawk.

The falcon eats other birds as well as small mammals. This gray-black bird hovers over the open grassland until it spots prey. Then it swoops down at amazing speeds of up to 150 miles per hour. With great accuracy, it grasps the prey in the sharp, curved, widely spread talons and at the same time kills it with a strike from one single rear talon. Sometimes the falcon will cripple the prey, return to the air, and then return later for the final kill.

Some falcons use other birds' nests instead of building their own. Some use woodpecker holes, while some take over crows' nests in trees. Some that build weak nests choose inaccessible cliff tops or just scoop out a hollow in open grassland.

Falcons tend to mate for life, which means that a pair of falcons will mate every year. The male swoops through the air displaying his flying skills while the female does most of the work looking after the eggs.

According to the Mosaic Law, the falcon is unclean and may not be eaten.

DID YOU KNOW...

- A falcon keeps its feathers clean by taking a bath in a stream.

- It takes a young falcon much practice and sometimes a long time to learn hunting skills.

- In a sport called "falconry," a falcon can be trained to take off from a person's wrist and hunt wild birds and small animals.

- Falcons are known as "birds of prey," also called "raptors."

49

FERRET

WHAT IS A "WEASEL WAR DANCE"?

Type of animal:
Mammal

Find it in the Bible:
Leviticus 11:30 KJV

The ferret is a member of the weasel family. It has a long body, short legs, and very sharp teeth. The ferret's fur is of various colors and patterns—white, black, silver, brown, albino, or mixed. It is nearsighted but has a good sense of hearing and smell.

The ferret spends fourteen to eighteen hours a day sleeping. When it is awake, it is energetic, curious, and interested in its surroundings. When a ferret gets excited, it will perform a "weasel war dance." The body becomes stiff, followed by thrashing and turning the head from side to side. The back arches, and the ferret hops from side to side and backward as it makes a soft clucking noise. During this "war dance," the ferret may bump into obstacles or trip over its own feet.

The ferret is born with scent glands, which it uses for self-defense. The glands give off a strong odor that frightens potential predators.

In years past, farmers used ferrets in their barns to help control rodents. Since a ferret has a long, lean build, it can easily slither into holes and chase rodents out of their burrows. Hunters have also used ferrets to hunt rabbits.

The ferret is listed in the Mosaic Law as an unclean animal. It is possible that people in biblical times used the animal for rodent control.

OTHER BIBLE TRANSLATIONS CALLED THIS ANIMAL "GECKO" OR "LIZARD."

DID YOU KNOW. . .

- A male ferret is called a "hob," and the female ferret is called a "jill."

- The ferret will carry small objects to secluded locations and hide them.

- A ferret makes a good pet, as it loves to play with humans.

FISH

LET'S GO FISHING!

Fish are cold-blooded animals (those whose body temperature changes with the temperature of their surroundings) that have fins to help them swim and gills they use to take in oxygen from the water. Most fish spend their entire lives in water, but some fish are able to live on land for short periods of time.

Most fish are designed for swimming. Their sleek, slender bodies glide through the water, and they use their fins for swimming. The size, shape, and number of fins depends on the species of fish. Each of the fins serves a different purpose.

Fish also use their strong muscles to help them swim. As they wiggle their body in an S-pattern, the tail presses against the water and pushes the fish forward.

Many fish have a sac inside their bodies called a "swim bladder." The gas inside the sac helps to keep the fish upright and to stay at a certain depth as it swims. Fish that live in the deep water do not have a swim bladder.

Most fish have scales covering their skin to protect their bodies. The scales are different colors, shapes, and sizes, depending on the species. Most fish have teeth suited to what they eat. Sharks eat other fish, so they need large, sharp teeth. Other fish have smaller teeth that help them eat their favorite food, plankton. Still other fish have no teeth at all!

Fish avoid or fight off their predators in many different ways. Some fish swim very fast and can simply outrun their enemies. Some fish use

Some fish, like these tropical fish that live near a coral reef, are beautifully colored.

51

During biblical times, fishermen used nets to catch their fish. In some parts of the world, fisherman still use nets to catch fish.

camouflage to protect themselves. Their coloring and shape help hide them in their surroundings. Other fish are poisonous. For example, a stingray attacks predators with a poisonous whiplike tail. Others have prickly poisonous spines, while others have poisonous flesh.

Some fish have a keen sense of smell in the water. For example, the salmon smells the water to know how to return to the same stream where it was born. Others smell the water to travel to the same grounds when they migrate.

Fish are mentioned often in the Bible but not by the different species. Fish abounded in the inland waters of Palestine, as well as in the Mediterranean Sea. As the Israelites ate manna in the wilderness, they remembered eating fish in Egypt (see Numbers 11:5). According to the Mosaic Law, all fish with fins and scales were clean, but those water animals with no fins or scales were unclean (Leviticus 11:9–12).

The Bible mentions several ways to catch fish. Fishing with a line and hook, harpooning, and spear fishing are all mentioned in Job 41:1 and 7. Casting a net into the water is mentioned in Matthew 4:18, and the use of large dragnets cast from a boat is mentioned in John 21:8.

Fish caught in the Mediterranean Sea were mostly brought to the ports of Tyre and Sidon. The Sea of Galilee was also a fishing center. The fish caught there were brought to Jerusalem to be sold at the Fish Gate in the city.

During New Testament times, commercial fishing businesses were conducted on the Sea of Galilee. Many fishermen owned their ships, and fish provided food for the people along the seaport.

The most famous biblical fish story is found in the Old Testament book of Jonah. God prepared a special fish to swallow Jonah when he would not obey Him.

OTHER BIBLE VERSES THAT MENTION FISH ARE 2 CHRONICLES 33:14; NEHEMIAH 3:3; PSALM 8:8; LUKE 24:42; AND JOHN 21:3-13.

Some of Jesus' disciples—Simon Peter, Andrew, James, and John—were fishermen by trade. Fish was a common food for Jesus and His disciples. The New Testament gives an account of Jesus feeding more than five thousand people with a boy's five loaves of bread and two fish (John 6:1–15).

DID YOU KNOW. . .

- There are about twenty-eight thousand different species of fish living around the world today.

- The fastest fish in the world is the sailfish, which has been known to swim at speeds of almost 70 miles per hour.

- Fish never close their eyes because they do not have eyelids.

- Some fish travel in groups called "schools."

- The archerfish can squirt a jet of water droplets at insects on leaves above the surface, knocking them into the water.

53

FLEA

WOW! LOOK AT THAT FLEA GO!

Type of animal:
Insect
Find it in the Bible:
1 Samuel 24:14

The flea is a tiny insect less than a quarter inch long. It has a flattened body that helps it wander between the hairs of the animal it rides on and feeds from. It has no wings but has large back legs with rubbery pads. The pads are squeezed tightly by muscles and keep packed together until the flea needs to jump. Then the pads are released, allowing the flea to spring onto a passing victim. It quickly scurries between hairs and grips the skin with needle-sharp claws. When it is ready to eat, the flea cuts the skin with mouthparts that are like jagged edges of a knife blade. The sharp beak enters the skin and injects a chemical that stops the blood from clotting. The host's body pumps the blood into the flea's stomach.

Most fleas do not carry dangerous diseases. But some carry diseases that can cause death. For example, the rat flea carries the bacteria that caused a disease known as the bubonic plague, which spread through Europe during the fourteenth century. This plague killed about half of Europe's population.

The flea was a plague for people and animals during Israel's early history. Some Bible scholars believe fleas were the carriers of the disease that fell upon the Assyrians during the ministry of the prophet Isaiah (see Isaiah 37:36–37). Also, David, before he became king of Israel, humbly compared himself to a flea when he spoke to King Saul (see 1 Samuel 24:14; 26:20).

Fleas would be scary looking if they weren't so tiny!

DID YOU KNOW. . .

- The flea is about the size of a pinhead.
- Fleas have been known to jump up to two hundred times their own body length.
- A flea does not live on humans, but comes, bites, and then leaves.

Type of animal:
Insect

Find it in the Bible:
Psalm 105:31

FLY

WAITER! THERE'S A FLY IN MY SOUP!

A fly has a mobile head, large compound eyes (eyes that are made up of many smaller eyes), and a single pair of wings. It has small, white knobs just behind its wings called "halters," which give it balance when it flies through the air. It also has sticky pads on its feet, which give it the ability to walk on the ceiling or hang from wires and branches. Flies are mostly inactive at night and more active during cooler rather than warm temperatures.

There are more than 120,000 species of flies, and they are found everywhere in the world except the supercold continent of Antarctica. The most common is the housefly, which is a pest that can carry disease-causing germs in its saliva and on its body.

The housefly is a scavenger that eats anything sugary or rotting that it can absorb with its spongy mouth pads. It uses its tongue, which is shaped like a straw, to suck up liquid food. The fly can easily eat liquid food, but eating solids like sugar is a little trickier for the fly because it doesn't have jaws or teeth. To eat solid food like sugar, the fly vomits saliva and digestive juices onto the meal then gives it a chance to dissolve. Then it gobbles up the liquefied meal with its tongue.

The female fly lays her eggs in rotting waste. She may lay up to five hundred eggs in several batches of seventy-five to one hundred eggs over a period of three or four days. The eggs must remain moist or they will not hatch. When the eggs hatch—usually within twenty-four hours—they produce larvae called "maggots." The maggots are active for two or three weeks, feasting on the same rotten stuff they were hatched in. Before long, the maggot becomes a pupa, which is the last step before it becomes an adult fly.

The fly mostly stays within one or two miles of where it was born, but it may travel as far as twenty miles to find food. One of the reasons flies are found where people are found is that they can easily find food.

WHAT A BORING LIFE!

Can you imagine having millions of these little pests flying around your neighborhood? That's what happened in Egypt when Pharaoh refused to let God's people go free!

A PLAGUE OF FLIES

Flies are first mentioned in the Bible in the eighth chapter of Exodus, which includes the plague of flies God sent to Egypt when Pharaoh refused to free the people of Israel from bondage.

Moses and his brother Aaron had gone to Pharaoh for the fourth time, and for the fourth time they told him, "God wants you to let His people go!" They also warned Pharaoh that God would send a plague of flies if he refused. But the stubborn Pharaoh would not let the Israelites go.

So God sent flies. Not just a few flies, but huge swarms of them. The air was literally black with the little pests. God did not allow the flies to bother the Israelites, but all of the Egyptians were swatting flies and trying to get away from them. But still Pharaoh was stubborn. "No! You may not go!" he shouted.

King David later recalled how God took care of His people when Pharaoh held them in bondage. He remembered the miraculous signs God performed in Egypt (including sending the flies!) before Pharaoh finally let the people go free

See Psalm 78:42–52

DID YOU KNOW. . .

- Houseflies have taste buds on their feet that allow them to taste sugar when they stand on it.
- A housefly can live only two or three days without food.
- Flies can beat their wings hundreds of times a second.
- The life cycle of a fly is short—an average of about twenty-one days.

Type of animal:
Mammal
Find it in the Bible:
Judges 15:4

FOX

YOU'RE A SLY OLD FOX!

The fox is the smallest member of the dog family. It has short legs, an extended narrow muzzle, erect triangular ears, thick fur, and a long, bushy tail. The red fox is the most common fox species. It has rusty red fur sprinkled with light-tipped hairs, black ears and feet, and a white-tipped tail.

The fox has a small, slender body that is designed for quickness. It can run as fast as 30 miles per hour. The fox is a shy, nervous hunter and scavenger that is most active at night. It will eat everything from insects to small mammals to berries to human garbage. Since the fox does not eat large prey, it hunts alone rather than in a pack.

When a lot of food is available, the fox will store it in shallow holes. It will make several storage places around its territory to prevent other animals from taking its food.

The fox has keen senses of smell, hearing, and sight. It can pick up low-frequency sounds, even the sound of an animal digging or scratching in an underground burrow. When the fox hears a mouse, it stands still and alert until it sees the prey. Then it launches at the prey, pinning it to the ground. If the fox is not hungry, it plays with the catch—just like cats sometimes do.

Red foxes pair for life with a mate. They make dens tucked away in rock crevices, in abandoned

The red fox is the most common species of fox in the world.

57

rabbit burrows, or in holes in trees. Foxes are very territorial and will defend their territory and families.

Foxes abound in Palestine and are mentioned several times in the Bible. Foxes were a threat to the vineyards, as they trampled down the fruit vines and bushes as they devoured the fruit. But foxes were also a help to the farmers because they hunted the rodents and rabbits that destroyed other crops.

NEHEMIAH BUILDS THE WALLS

Nehemiah heard that the walls of the city of Jerusalem were broken down and the gates had been burned. He was sad and asked the king if he could go help rebuild the walls. The king told Nehemiah to go help.

Nehemiah gathered some men together and said, "Let's rebuild the walls. We will make them strong."

Some men were not pleased when they heard the walls were going to be rebuilt. They did not like Nehemiah and the Jews. One of the men, named Sanballat, said, "Do these weak Jews think they can make their city strong?"

Tobiah, his servant, was with him and also made fun of the men and their work. He said, "If a fox would climb up the wall, it would break down."

The enemy tried to form an army to fight Nehemiah and keep the walls from being built. But Nehemiah prayed and asked God to help them build the wall of Jerusalem. God heard Nehemiah's prayer.

Foxes make their dens in all kinds of places. This young fox lives in a hole under an oak tree.

You can read the whole story in Nehemiah 4. Foxes are also mentioned in the New Testament, in Luke 9. One day a man came to Jesus and said that he wanted to follow Him. Jesus told the man, "Foxes have holes and birds of the air have nests, but the Son of Man has no place to lay his head" (Luke 9:58 NIV).

THE FIERY FOXES

Samson went to see his wife, but her father would not let him into the house to see her. Samson became angry. "I will get even with them," Samson said to himself.

Samson went out and caught three hundred foxes and tied them together in pairs by their tails. Then he tied a piece of wood between the tails. When the Philistine's grain was ready to harvest, Samson lit the wood and let the foxes loose. They ran into the fields of grain and burned up the shocks and grain, along with the vineyards and olive groves (see Judges 15:1–8).

Some Bible scholars believe that the foxes mentioned in this story were actually jackals. That's because foxes are solitary animals while jackals run in packs and hide in caves, which would have made them easier for Samson to catch. But most of the translations of the Bible use the word foxes in the story.

DID YOU KNOW...

- The red fox is about the size of a large cat.

- A fox's hearing is so good that it can hear a watch ticking forty yards away.

- The gray fox is the only fox species that can climb trees.

- The fox's average lifespan is about twelve years.

Samson was tough, but dumb...even though he burned the Philistines' fields with flaming foxes, he fell in love with a Philistine woman, Delilah—who led to his death in a Philistine temple.

FROG

IS IT TRUE
THAT FROGS
HAVE TEETH?

Type of animal:

Amphibian

Find it in the Bible:

Exodus 8:6

Frogs are known for their short bodies, long hind legs, webbed toes, bulgy eyes, and by the fact that they don't have a tail. Frogs have very strong hind legs, which give them amazing jumping ability. Most frogs spend the majority of their time in water, but they can also move easily on land by jumping, crawling, or climbing.

A frog must be able to move quickly to catch prey and to escape predators. Some frogs use their sticky tongues to catch their food. All frogs are carnivorous, which means that they eat other animals. Most of them eat small prey such as insects and other bugs. But some frogs eat small fish, reptiles, and animals. Some frogs like to eat. . .other frogs!

The frog has a ridge of very small teeth around the upper edge of the jaw and teeth on the roof of its mouth. It doesn't use its teeth to chew but to keep a good grip on its prey, which it swallows whole. When the frog swallows a meal, it closes its bulgy eyeballs as it pushes its food down its throat.

A frog begins its life as an egg its mother laid in a pond, puddle, or lake. When the baby frog hatches, it isn't yet a frog but a tadpole, which looks like a little fish and breathes with gills like a fish. As the tadpole feasts on algae and other plant life, it undergoes some big changes. It begins to grow back legs then front legs. The gills are replaced by lungs, and the digestive system changes so that the adult frog can begin life as a meat eater. The last step toward maturity is the disappearance of the tail, which is absorbed into the frog's body.

There are thousands of species of frogs living wherever it's warm enough and wet enough for frogs to live. They come in many different colors and sizes.

This animal is mentioned several times in the Old Testament, including the account of Moses and the ten plagues on Egypt.

From tadpole to frog. . .the transformation is almost complete!

THE PLAGUE OF THE FROGS

Moses had returned to Pharaoh when he would not let the Israelites go after the first plague—when the water in Egypt turned to blood (Exodus 7:19). "God will cover the land with frogs if you will not let the people go," Moses warned Pharaoh.

But Pharaoh would not let the people go. So, just as God had promised, swarms of frogs entered the houses and the land. They were everywhere!

CAN YOU IMAGINE FINDING A FROG ON YOUR BED?

Then Pharaoh said, "Tell God to take the frogs away. I will let the people go."

Moses told Pharaoh the frogs would go away. But do you think that sly old pharaoh let the Israelites go? Read the whole story in Exodus 8 and find out!

Other Bible verses that mention frogs are Psalm 78:45 and 105:30.

DID YOU KNOW. . .

- Some frogs can jump more than twenty times their length, which is about like you jumping one hundred feet.
- The Goliath frog is nearly a foot long with legs that long, too.
- The adult gold frog is only three-eighths of an inch long.
- In captivity, some frogs have been known to live as long as forty years.

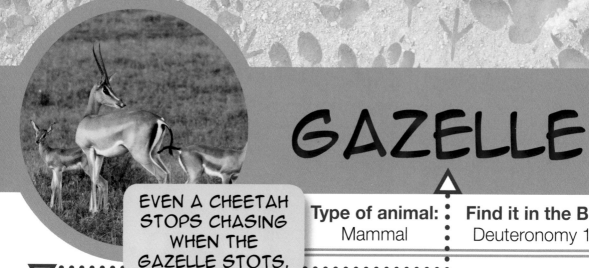

GAZELLE

EVEN A CHEETAH STOPS CHASING WHEN THE GAZELLE STOTS.

Type of animal:
Mammal

Find it in the Bible:
Deuteronomy 14:5

The graceful, speedy gazelle is a species of antelope. It is light brown in color with a white underbelly. It has black and white markings on its face with a horizontal dark band along each side. It has long, pointed ears, large eyes, and V-shaped antlers that extend backward from its head.

Some gazelles live in the mountainous regions, but most graze on grassy plains with very few places to hide. Life on the plains exposes the gazelle to predators such as lions, leopards, and wild dogs. Its antlers offer no protection, so it relies on its speed to elude its enemies. Gazelles are very fast.

The gazelle has a clever way of dealing with its enemies. It is called "stotting." The gazelle leaps high in the air with all four legs stiff and back arched as if to say, "I see you! Don't sneak up on me!" It sometimes does this while an enemy is chasing it. It often works as the enemy breaks off the chase.

Gazelles live in herds, and that offers them some protection against predators. When one gazelle in the herd senses danger, it wiggles its white rump to tell the other gazelles of the threat.

According to Mosaic Law, the gazelle is considered clean, which means it was permitted as food for the people of Israel. The gazelle has divided hooves and chews the cud.

DID YOU KNOW. . .

- The gazelle can run as fast as 50 miles per hour.
- To reach leaves on a tree to eat, the gazelle stands on its hind legs and stretches its long neck.
- The gazelle has little need for drinking water, because it gets most of its moisture from plants.

Type of animal:

Reptile

Find it in the Bible:

Leviticus 11:30

GECKO

OH, WHAT BIG EYES YOU HAVE!

The gecko is a lizard that comes in a variety of colors and patterns. Some are delicately patterned and rubbery looking, while others are brightly colored. Some species even change colors to blend in with their surroundings. The different color patterns help camouflage the gecko from its enemies.

The gecko has a triangular head and a large tail where it stores fat. It can break off its tail when threatened, leaving a predator with nothing but a tail in its mouth as the lizard scurries away to safety. Its skin is bumpy. It has huge eyes and sees very well—especially at night, when it is most active. The gecko's toes have brushlike foot pads on them that hold them to most surfaces. This makes it easy for them to climb walls and walk across ceilings.

SOME VERSIONS OF THE BIBLE CALL THIS ANIMAL A FERRET, BUT LATER SCHOLARS BELIEVE "GECKO" IS THE CORRECT TRANSLATION.

The gecko is harmless to humans and is in fact welcomed in homes in some parts of the world because it feeds on annoying insects such as mosquitoes, which it swallows whole.

The gecko is the only reptile that has the ability to use its voice (other than the hissing sounds some reptiles make). It often makes barking, chirping, and clicking noises when it interacts with fellow geckoes.

The gecko mentioned in the Bible is probably the fan-foot gecko, which is common in Egypt and in parts of Arabia, and might also be found in Palestine. It is reddish brown with white spots. It is considered unclean according to Mosaic Law.

DID YOU KNOW. . .

- The gecko gets its name from the peculiar sound it makes: "geck-oh, geck-oh, geck-oh."
- The gecko's feet are self-cleaning and will usually remove clogged dirt within a few steps.
- The gecko makes a good pet—if you like lizards, that is!

The design of the gecko's toes allows the lizard to cling to nearly any surface.

63

GNAT

WHAT'S THAT CLOUD OF SMOKE COMING AT ME?

A gnat is a tiny flying insect with two wings, jointed legs, large eyes, and long hairlike antennae. The body is often covered with soft hairlike strands. There are several species of gnats. Some gnats use their snout for piercing and sucking. The female gnat will bite and suck a tiny bit of blood, which she uses to feed her eggs.

Gnats are barely visible to the human eye, but some kinds of gnats leave a bite that stings and burns. The buffalo gnat, with its humpbacked appearance, can inflict painful bites on humans. Swarms of buffalo gnats have been known to kill farm animals with their bites. Most gnats are pests and cause damage to plants, especially flowering plants. Some gnat larva feed on the roots of potted flowering plants.

Gnats often come together in large groups called "swarms." They hang in the air like a cloud of smoke. The gnat usually lives alone, but during mating season, the males gather, especially at dusk, in large swarms called "ghosts." If a female approaches the ghost, one of the males will quickly approach her, and they will fly away together to mate. If the weather changes or a breeze blows, the ghost breaks up.

Some species of gnats fly at night, while others fly in the day, mainly in shaded areas. Still others attack in the bright sunlight.

The Old Testament writers knew about gnats and considered them pests. Because of the disease and damage the tiny insects can cause, many scholars identified the Egyptian plague as being gnats instead of lice, as is used in the King James Version (Exodus 8:16–19). David also wrote about the swarm of gnats God sent as a plague on Pharaoh and the Egyptian people (Psalm 105:31).

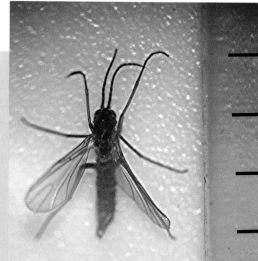

The fungus gnat is a pest because its larvae feed on plant roots and mushrooms.

THE THIRD PLAGUE

God had earlier sent Moses to ask Pharaoh to let His people, the Israelites, go free from slavery. He had sent the plague that changed the water into blood, but Pharaoh would not let the people go. God had sent the frogs that covered the land. Still Pharaoh said, "No!"

Again God sent Moses to Pharaoh. "If you do not let the people go, God will send a swarm of gnats," Moses warned Pharaoh.

So God sent the swarm of gnats to cover the land, the people, and the animals. But Pharaoh's heart was hardened and he would not listen to Moses.

See Exodus 8:16–19

Can you imagine being surrounded by millions of insects like this one that wanted to bite you? The people of Egypt found out just how that felt!

DID YOU KNOW. . .

- A swarm of gnats can include as many as a million individuals.
- The larvae of some species of gnats live in the water and provide food for aquatic life.
- A gnat flies in circles because its right and left wings are different sizes.
- Several tiny species of gnats are called "midges."

GOAT

A GOAT WILL NOT EAT A TIN CAN!

Type of animal:
Mammal
Find it in the Bible:
2 Chronicles 29:23

The goat is one of the oldest domesticated animals. The most common goat has long, floppy ears and is usually covered with long black hair. Some goats don't have horns, but different species have horns of various shapes and sizes. Both male and female have a wattle, a flap of skin that hangs from under their necks.

The goat is useful to humans in several ways. Goat's milk is used for drinking and for making butter and cheese. In some parts of the world, goat's meat is eaten. Also, the goat's intestines are used to make the strings on music instruments, and its horns are carved into spoons. Once or twice a year, farmers shear goats for the wool. Angora goats produce long, curling, glistening locks of mohair. Cashmere goats produce cashmere wool, which is a valuable natural fiber. Both are used to make clothing.

A WATTLE IS A FLAP OF SKIN HANGING FROM UNDER THE NECK.

This pygmy goat has found the grass greener on the other side of the fence. And, no, he isn't looking for tin cans to eat!

Contrary to what many people think, goats don't like to eat tin cans, clothing, or garbage. They are actually very picky eaters when they are provided a well-balanced diet. The goat's four-chamber stomach breaks down any organic substance, providing the animal with the nutrients it needs.

Goats prefer to eat the tips of woody shrubs and trees. Sometimes they stand on their back feet to reach leaves on low tree branches. They also browse on grass and weeds, including certain plants that are poisonous to other animals. Goats can be very destructive to vegetation because they tear plants out of the soil by the roots when they eat. This can contribute to erosion.

A goat is a social animal. It is lively, curious, and independent. It explores anything new in its surroundings.

Sometimes it nibbles with its tongue and upper lip to check out items such as buttons or clothing made with plant or wood fibers.

The goat can easily be trained to pull carts and walk on a leash, but it is a great "escape artist." It can open gates and push down or climb over any weak fence. It can jump as high as five feet, so it is difficult to keep a goat in a penned area.

When the male goat, which is called a "buck," is ready to mate, he goes through a period called "rut." During this time, he has a decreased appetite, fights with other bucks, is obsessive with does, and gives off a strong, musky odor.

PEW! WHAT IS THAT STRONG SMELL?

The Bible mentions goats as being a hardy animal that can live nearly anywhere, even in the hot deserts of the Holy Land where there is very little plant life. A shepherd in biblical times treasured the goat because each doe provided him and his family with a gallon or more of milk each day. The goat's milk was also used to make cheese, yogurt, and butter. Each spring the shepherd cut the hair from their goats so it could be woven into water-resistant tents, cloaks, carpets, sacks, and even ropes. The hide was dried in the sun and then sewed into sandals and sturdy bags to hold water or wine. Goat meat was a source of food for the herder and his family.

Goats and sheep grazed in the same field. Many times the shepherd had to separate the herds because the male goats were sometimes hostile toward the sheep. The shepherd also kept the herd of goats moving so they wouldn't gobble up all the plants and pull the roots from the ground. Vegetation would not grow back when the roots were destroyed. Since goats were sometimes stubborn and troublesome, the shepherd had to keep them from wandering away from the herd.

If you ever get close enough to a goat, you might find he's more curious about you than you are about him!

Male goats were used for sacrifices in the Old Testament. When Abraham received a covenant from God, the goat was among the animals he sacrificed to God (see Genesis 15:9). Samson's

GOAT

Like sheep, goats were important animals to people living in biblical times. Shepherds often cared for both sheep and goats.

parents sacrificed a goat to God as an angel talked to them about raising their son (see Judges 13:19).

In the Mosaic Law, a male goat without defect (meaning it was perfect in every way) was among the burnt offerings that Israelites were to sacrifice for their sins (Leviticus 4:24 and 16:15). The priests under King Hezekiah offered goats at the temple as a sin offering (2 Chronicles 29:23).

During Old Testament times, two goats were brought to the altar of God once a year on the Day of Atonement. One goat was dedicated and sacrificed to God. The priest laid his hands on the second goat and spoke the sins of the people. This goat was sent into the wilderness as a symbol of sending sin away from the people of God. That goat was called the "scapegoat."

DID YOU KNOW. . .

- The male goat is called a "billy" or "buck," the female is called a "doe" or "nanny," and the baby goat is called a "kid."

- A goat can go as long as two weeks without water.

- In certain circumstances, the goat has the ability to climb trees.

- A goat does not like to get wet and will seek shelter when it is raining.

- A goat's hooves are used to make gelatin.

GRASSHOPPER

Type of animal: Insect

Find it in the Bible: Numbers 13:33

HOW ABOUT A CRUNCHY CHOCOLATE GRASSHOPPER?

The grasshopper is a common insect that feeds on plants. It has a slender body, powerful hind legs, short antennae, and two pairs of well-developed wings. Its narrow, leathery forewings have markings that help camouflage this insect. Its large hind wings are much thinner and can open out like fans, which help propel the grasshopper into flight. The grasshopper usually moves by jumping, but it flies when it needs to get somewhere fast or when it needs to escape predators.

The grasshopper uses its long, slender hind legs for jumping. If a predator grabs the grasshopper by a leg, it can shed its leg rather than being caught and eaten. A special lining quickly seals the wound so not much blood is lost. The grasshopper can still jump with only one hind leg.

The grasshopper has three ways to survive attacks from predators. It will hop or fly away when possible. Also, with its green or brown coloring, it can blend into its surroundings. Finally, it spits a smelly brown juice when it is threatened.

WITH LEGS LIKE THOSE, THIS GRASSHOPPER SHOULD BE A WORLD-CLASS JUMPER!

In some grasshopper species, the process of mating begins when the male attracts the female by rubbing his legs against his wings to make music. After mating, the female grasshopper drills a hole in the ground and lays her eggs, using a tube-like appendage called an "ovipositor." The eggs, which are laid in small pods that contain several dozen, stay in the ground during the winter and hatch in the spring.

When the young grasshoppers begin to hatch, they tunnel out of the ground and then begin to develop into adult grasshoppers. Grasshoppers live only a few months after they hatch. During their short lifetime, they eat, grow, reproduce, and then die. Since so many animals—including birds, reptiles, fish, and mammals—like to eat grasshoppers, many of them end up being someone else's dinner and never have the chance to reproduce.

Grasshoppers can be found just about anywhere they can find enough green plants to eat.

Can you see the green grasshopper hiding in the grass? Maybe a predator won't see him either!

DID YOU KNOW. . .

- The grasshopper can jump twenty times the length of its body.

- The young grasshopper does not have wings but develops them later as an adult.

- The grasshopper is of great value because it provides food for many people.

Grasshoppers are eating machines! In large numbers, they have been known to destroy entire crops of grass, alfalfa, clover, cotton, corn, and other valuable crops.

According to the Mosaic Law, grasshoppers are clean and can be eaten (Leviticus 11:21–22). Grasshoppers are also mentioned in the Bible in reference to their size. Ten of the twelve spies who went to check out Canaan saw themselves as grasshoppers when compared to the giant inhabitants of Canaan (see Numbers 13:26–33).

Type of animal:

Bird

Find it in the Bible:

Deuteronomy 14:15

GULL

WOW! LOOK AT THOSE BRIGHT PINK LEGS!

The gull, which is most often called a "seagull," is a seabird found along coasts. There are many kinds of gulls, but most of them have mainly white plumage with gray or black markings on the wings. The gull's wings, which help the bird soar through the air, are narrow and long, and its feet are webbed like a duck's for swimming. The gull has a bright orange spot on the lower part of its beak. The beak is powerful and has a hooked tip used for tearing up pieces of food and defending the bird against attackers. When a gull is resting, it folds its wings over its back.

While gulls are seabirds in nature, they are now often found inland, where they can scavenge through garbage dumps and other places to find leftover food that people discard. Gulls also often follow large ships at sea so they can find food by picking through waste thrown overboard.

Gulls will eat a wide variety of foods, but they prefer meat and fish. In the wild, they catch fish and other marine creatures—such as crustaceans and shellfish—that live in the water and along the shoreline.

Some gulls have learned a trick that helps them to eat the best tidbits from the marine creatures they catch. They drop hard-shelled clams and sea urchins onto hard surfaces to crack them open. In the winter, they drop mussels onto the ice to crack them.

Most gulls nest once a year in large, noisy colonies. After mating, the female lays two or three speckled eggs in her nest, which is built on the ground out of vegetation. The young are born with dark, mottled down instead of feathers. Mother gulls are known to be very protective of their eggs and babies.

The gull is listed in the Mosaic Law as an unclean bird, meaning the Israelites were not to eat it.

DID YOU KNOW. . .

- Some gulls build their nests on inland rooftops.

- Herring gulls have bright pink legs!

- Food gulls cannot digest, such as fish bones and crab claws, is spit out in pellets.

71

HAWK

WHAT WAS THAT STREAKING ACROSS THE SKY?

Type of animal:
Bird
Find it in the Bible:
Job 39:26

The hawk is a bird of prey (a meat eater that catches its own food) with short, rounded wings and a long tail—both of which it uses to fly swiftly. It has a hooked beak and sharp talon feet. It captures and kills its prey with its claws and then tears it apart with its beak.

There are many species of hawks, and they vary in their hunting habits. The marsh hawk uses its sense of hearing to listen for snakes and rodents as it silently flies low over marshlands. The crane hawk has double-jointed legs that can bend both backward and forward to catch small mammals sheltering in cracks of cliffs.

Seeing prey from the air, the northern goshawk folds its wings to its side, maneuvers with its long tail, and follows the prey through the trees and bushes. The red-shouldered hawk sits quietly on a low-lying perch, waiting and watching for prey, and then swoops down on it.

Different species of hawks have different mating habits. Red-tailed hawks, which mate for life, fly at great heights during courtship—up to two hundred feet. The male then does a steep dive toward the ground. He repeats this several times before he approaches the female from above to touch her or grasp her in midair.

The hawk is listed in the Mosaic Law as an unclean animal, which means Israelites were forbidden to eat it (Leviticus 11:16).

WHAT A CLOWN!

DID YOU KNOW. . .

- Some hawks can fly as fast as 150 miles per hour.
- A hawk's eyesight is eight times better than a human's eyesight.
- The male hawk brings food to the female while she sits on her nest, but she must catch it as he drops it from the air.

HEDGEHOG

Type of animal:
Mammal

Find it in the Bible:
Isaiah 14:23 RSV

WHAT A PRICKLY BALL!

The hedgehog has a sharp narrow snout, small eyes, and short legs. It has weak eyesight but has excellent hearing and smell. Its face, legs, tail, and belly are covered with fur, but its back and sides are covered with smooth spines.

The hedgehog's spines are hollow but not barbed like the porcupine's spines. The adult hedgehog loses its spines only when it is stressed or sick. Young hedgehogs shed their baby spines and grow adult spines in their place. This is called "quilling." The adult male hedgehog may have as many as five hundred spines.

Other than running away, the hedgehog's spines are its primary defense against predators. After first trying to run from a predator, the hedgehog rolls its body into a tight ball, causing the spines to point outward. That leaves the predator no place to catch hold or attack.

The hedgehog sleeps a large portion of the day under a bush, rock, or hole in the ground. It curls up in a ball as it sleeps. It awakens at night to hunt for frogs, lizards, bird eggs, worms, snails, and insects. It will also eat mushrooms, as well as berries and other fruit.

Hedgehogs aren't found in the wild in the United States, but people sometimes keep them as pets. They live in the wild in Europe, Asia, Africa, and New Zealand. They are valuable to humans because they eat large numbers of pests that are harmful to gardens.

The Bible mentions hedgehogs only twice. The prophets Isaiah (14:23) and Zephaniah (2:14 RSV) wrote of the hedgehog as living in a desolate place.

DID YOU KNOW...

- The hedgehog sometimes performs a ritual known as "anointing." When it comes upon a new scent, it will lick the source. Then the hedgehog will form a scented froth in its mouth and paste it on its spines with its long tongue.

- The baby hedgehog begins developing quills within an hour after it is born.

- The hedgehog gets its name "hedge" because it moves through hedges and "hog" because of its piglike snout.

73

HEN & CHICKS

THOSE LITTLE CHICKS ARE SO SOFT AND FLUFFY.

Type of animal: Bird

Find it in the Bible: Luke 13:34

The hen—the name for a female chicken—has a solid body, sturdy legs, soft feet, and a short, pointed beak. Her short wings are not useful for continuous flight, but smaller, lighter hens can fly (or glide) short distances over a fence or into a tree. The hen has a fleshy red growth on her head called a "comb."

If a hen is allowed to run free, she will eat grains, insects, worms, and other sources of food she finds. Domesticated hens, which are important sources of meat and eggs for humans, are usually fed prepared chicken feed.

Even though domesticated hens lay eggs just like any other hen, most of them won't sit on them until they hatch. Once they have laid their eggs, they leave them behind to be gathered up for food for people.

Hens that sit on their eggs until they hatch usually lay one egg a day until there are ten to twelve eggs in the nest. The hen then stops laying eggs and begins spending most of her time on the nest until the chicks are ready to hatch—usually three weeks.

Before an egg hatches, the hen hears the chick peeping from inside the egg. She will gently cluck to the chick, encouraging it to break out of the shell. The chick first pecks a breathing hole in the egg's shell. After resting a few hours, the chick pecks open the egg and crawls out. The chick is wet when it first hatches, but it dries quickly in the warmth of the nest.

The hen guards her chicks from predators and leads them to places where they can find water and food. She also takes them under her wings at night to keep them warm.

The hen and chicks are mentioned just two times in the Bible, but the birds must have been common in Palestine. In the New Testament, Jesus compared Himself to a mother hen as He grieved over the wayward city of Jerusalem. Just as a mother hen gathers her chicks under her wing to protect them, Jesus wanted to gather His people in Jerusalem and care for them and protect them (see Matthew 23:37).

DID YOU KNOW. . .

- The hen is a female chicken.
- A hen will usually live five to eleven years, depending on the breed.
- The world's oldest hen died of heart failure when she was sixteen years old.

Type of animal:

Bird

Find it in the Bible:

Deuteronomy 14:18

HERON

WHAT IS POWDER DOWN?

The heron is a medium- to large-sized wading bird with a long neck and legs. It has long, thin toes—three of which point forward and one backward—on its feet. It is a meat-eating bird that feeds around water, catching fish, amphibians, reptiles, crustaceans, mollusks, small birds, and aquatic insects.

The heron hunts by standing by the water and waiting to ambush unsuspecting prey. When a fish or frog comes along, the heron spears the victim with its long, sharp bill. It usually swallows the prey whole.

Some species of herons gather in groups or colonies and build bulky stick nests in trees, while others tend to nest in reed beds by the water.

The heron has a strangely shaped sixth vertebra in its neck, which allows it to kink its neck into an S-shape. Unlike other long-necked birds, such as the stork or ibis, the heron flies with its neck retracted instead of stretched out. It also holds its legs and feet backward when it flies.

The heron is the only species of wading bird that has powder down on its body. Powder down is a layer of fine feathers found under tougher exterior feathers. The young birds are clad in all down.

There are more than sixty species of herons, each with different feathers and plumage. The egret is a small member of the heron family with mainly white feathers and some decorative plumes. The great blue heron is a large bluish gray bird with a black plume extending from behind the eye to the back of the neck. The black night heron is small with a shorter neck than most herons. It has a black crown and back with a white or gray body and red eyes.

Nearly all known species of herons are found in the vicinity of Palestine. They are listed in the Mosaic Law as unclean birds.

DID YOU KNOW. . .

● The gray (or grey) heron has a wingspan of up to six feet.

● Pillows are sometimes made from the "powder down" of a heron.

● The heron makes a harsh croak and is quite vocal during mating season.

HOOPOE

Type of animal:
Bird

Find it in the Bible:
Leviticus 11:19 NIV

The hoopoe is a colorful bird found across Africa and Asia. It has a cinnamon-colored body and black and white wings. It has a crown of feathers on its head that rises when it eats. When the hoopoe is not feeding, the feathered crest is flat and tilted back. The adult hoopoe stands ten to twelve inches tall.

The hoopoe forages on the ground, looking for insects, small reptiles, and frogs to eat. When it finds an insect, it inserts its bill into the ground. The muscles of the head allow the hoopoe to open its long, thin, tapering black bill. The hoopoe uses its bill to pull the insect out of the ground, but it sometimes uses its strong feet to dig it out. Sometimes the hoopoe beats larger prey against the ground or a rock in order to kill it and to remove uneatable parts such as wings and legs. Occasionally it feeds in the air on swarming insects.

This bird builds its nest in hidden hollows and cracks of trees and rock crevices. The hoopoe is known for its terrible housekeeping. The nests are filthy and smell very bad. That is because the bird doesn't remove its dung from the nest and because the female releases a musty-smelling substance from her preen gland when she is disturbed. The smell helps keep predators away. When an enemy approaches the nest, even the young birds will lift their rears and shoot a load of stinking droppings into the enemy's face.

Mosaic Law lists the hoopoe as an unclean bird that is not to be eaten. Even though the bird is called a "hoopoe" in modern Bible translations, the name is uncertain. It is called a "lapwing" in the King James Bible and a "waterhen" and "woodcock" in other translations.

DID YOU KNOW. . .?

- The hoopoe is an excellent runner.
- The hoopoe calls out, "Oop-oop-oop," during the mating season.
- The hoopoe enjoys taking dust and sand baths.

HORNET

Type of animal:
Insect

Find it in the Bible:
Exodus 23:28

OUCH! THAT STING HURTS!

The hornet is a type of wasp, a social insect (one that lives in colonies with others of its kind) known best for its ability to dish out painful stings. Depending on the species, a hornet can measure from half an inch long to over two inches long. The hornet has deeply indented, C-shaped eyes. The wings are reddish orange, and the abdomen is orange with a brown strip across its middle.

In spring, the queen hornet, who has already mated, builds a nest of chewed tree bark. She selects a dark sheltered place and builds a nest of individual hexagonal (six-sided) cells. The queen lays an egg in each cell. After five to eight days, the eggs hatch and become larvae. This first generation is made up of female workers who take over the queen's job of building nests and feeding the larvae.

At the end of the summer, the queen produces the first individuals capable of reproducing—both female and male. The males don't take part in nest building or repair or in the care of the larvae. Their only purpose is to mate with the queens during what are called "nuptial flights" and then die. The workers and the queens survive until late autumn when the workers die. Only the fertilized queens survive the winter. In the spring, they perform the same tasks their mothers did the year before.

Though the hornet's sting is painful—and sometimes dangerous—this insect is actually beneficial to humans because it helps keep the populations of some kinds of pests under control. Hornets hunt flies, wasps, bees, beetles, grasshoppers, caterpillars, and spiders.

Hornets are mentioned in the Old Testament as one of God's instruments for driving Israel's enemies out of Canaan (see Exodus 23:28).

DID YOU KNOW. . .

- Late in the summer, a hornet colony may include seven hundred workers.

- A hornet's sting is painful to humans, but some stings can cause dangerous allergic reactions.

- At more than two inches long, the Asian giant hornet, which has a dangerous sting, is the largest hornet species.

HORSE

HOW MANY NAMES DOES A HORSE HAVE?

Type of animal:
Mammal
Find it in the Bible
Exodus 14:9

The horse is a solid-hoofed animal that is important to people in many ways. People use horses for pleasure riding, sports competitions, entertainment, police work, agriculture, and several other purposes. In the past, horses were a primary source of transportation and were also used in warfare.

With its well-developed sense of balance, the horse can walk, trot, canter, and gallop. The horse walks at about 4 miles per hour and gallops at average speeds of between 25 and 30 miles per hour.

The horse is a very intelligent, trainable animal that has five highly developed senses. The eyes are larger than any other land animal, giving the horse the ability to see in nearly all directions. It has excellent day-night vision. Horses can also see color, even though they distinguish colors differently than humans. The horse also has a keen sense of smell.

A young foal relaxes in the grass, knowing mom is nearby. Mother horses are very tender and very protective of their young.

The horse's tail is important for several reasons. Not only is it used to swat flies, but also to keep the horse's "behind" warm during cold weather. Horses also use their tails to signal each other about how they are feeling.

Horses are plant eaters with digestive systems designed to handle grasses and grains. Horses have relatively small stomachs, so they must eat steadily throughout the day. A horse weighing around 950 pounds eats around 24 pounds of food and drinks about eight gallons of water each day. Horses do not "chew the cud" like cattle.

A male horse is called a "stallion," and a female is called a "mare." A father horse is called a "sire," and a mother horse is called a "dam." A horse just born is called a "foal." A boy foal is a "colt," and a girl foal is called a "filly."

There are currently about three hundred different breeds of horses. The different breeds of horses are identified through the color of their hair and skin, through their size, and through their physical abilities, such as strength and speed.

The average life span of a horse is about twenty-five to thirty years. "Old Billy," a horse that lived in England, was the oldest recorded horse on record—sixty-two years!

Horses are mentioned many times in the Bible. In Old Testament times, horses pulled chariots. Pharaoh and his men rode in chariots as they pursued the Israelites during the time of the Exodus. In later years, Egypt was the main source for the supply of horses used by the kings of Israel.

In biblical times, the horse was a "weapon" of war and stood for power. David made reference to using horses in battle. In his victory over the king of Zobah, David captured the chariots and let the horses go free. He kept a hundred of the horses for use in battle on the flat ground of his country (see 2 Samuel 8:1–4).

King Solomon gained a great supply of horses through his trade with Egypt. He built stables with stalls for the horses. Solomon established a very active trade in horses he imported from Egypt and resold to make a profit. An imported chariot cost six hundred shekels of silver, and a horse cost one hundred fifty shekels (see 1 Kings 10:29).

Kings or men of wealth or position were the main users of horse-drawn chariots. They rode in chariots covered with embroidered trappings or paraded around in royal robes on their decorated horses.

Though horses and chariots were used for war in biblical times, today they are used for sport and recreation.

DID YOU KNOW . . .

- A horse can sleep both standing up and lying down.
- Most foals are born at night when there is less activity.
- When a horse is born, its legs are almost their full adult length.
- Horses like calm or cheerful music, but loud music makes them uneasy.

HYENA

WHO IS THAT LAUGHING?

Type of animal:
Mammal
Find it in the Bible
1 Samuel 13:18 MSG

The hyena is a hunter and scavenger with a broad head, large eyes, and pointed ears. The hyena's front legs are longer than the rear ones, so it walks and runs awkwardly. The mane on the back of its neck is long and stands erect when the animal is frightened.

The hyena's coat coloring depends on the species. The aardwolf, striped hyena, and brown hyena all have striped pelts. The spotted hyena's fur is shorter and spotted instead of striped.

The hyena uses its bushy tail to communicate with other hyenas. The hyena holds its tail high when it is ready to attack. It holds its tail over its back when it is excited but tucks it between its back legs when it is frightened.

Hyenas also communicate with wailing calls and howling screams. The spotted hyena makes a haunting laughterlike call much like the laughter of a human. This call can be heard from as far away as three miles.

INSTEAD OF "VALLEY OF HYENAS," THE KING JAMES VERSION AND NEW INTERNATIONAL VERSION OF THE BIBLE USE THE TITLE "VALLEY OF ZEBOIM" IN 1 SAMUEL 13:18.

Most hyenas hunt in packs and run their prey down by exhaustion. Hyenas also eat the "leftovers" of dead animals killed by other predators.

The hyena's jaws are very strong. The animal's amazing digestive system allows it to eat and digest the entire prey—skin, teeth, horns, hooves, and bones. The only part it cannot digest is the hair. It coughs up the hair, which is known as a "hyena hair ball."

Hyenas are mentioned several times in The Message paraphrase of the Bible. First Samuel 13:18 mentions the Valley of Hyenas. It is assumed the valley was named for the animal that resided there. Hyenas are also mentioned in the same paraphrase in Isaiah 13:22 and 34:14 and in Jeremiah 15:3.

The hyena was regarded as a repulsive creature because it sometimes dug up dead bodies in Palestine.

DID YOU KNOW...

- The spotted hyena, which is mostly a predator, is also known as the "laughing hyena."

- The hyena can go for several days without water.

- The hyena can be dangerous to people and very destructive.

Type of animal:

Mammal

Find it in the Bible:

Deuteronomy 14:5

IBEX

THOSE HORNS ARE BIGGER THAN THE IBEX!

The ibex is a type of wild mountain goat. It has a heavy, stocky body and short, sturdy legs. The male ibex has a long pointed beard and a dark brown coat with a black stripe down its back and up the front of each foreleg. It has extremely large horns for its size. The horns sweep upward and backward in a semicircular direction and have knobby ridges across the outer surface of the curve. The female has a tan coat and smaller, thinner, straighter horns.

The ibex has a unique hoof structure that makes it an excellent climber on steep rocks and rocky ledges. Its even-toed hooves have hard edges and soft rubbery centers, which give the ibex a good grip on slippery rocks. Being able to climb to great heights helps protect the ibex from predators, because it can't be followed by other animals.

With keen sight and smell, the ibex is alert to any danger. It uses its horns as defense against predators. If the ibex senses danger, it raises its hind legs and points its horns toward the predator.

The Nubian ibex is the only species that adapts to the desert conditions of Bible lands. In fact, this animal is still found in the mountainous areas of Israel, Jordan, Saudi Arabia, Egypt, Yemen, and Sudan. The adult Nubian ibex stands about two feet tall at the shoulder and weights about 110 pounds. Its pale, shiny coat reflects sun rays and keeps it cool, even in the hot afternoon sun. It is active during the day and rests at night in the high sloping areas.

IN SOME BIBLE TRANSLATIONS, "WILD GOAT" IS USED INSTEAD OF "IBEX." BIBLE VERSES IN WHICH "WILD GOAT" IS USED ARE 1 SAMUEL 24:2 AND PSALM 104:18. IN THE KING JAMES VERSION, DEUTERONOMY 14:5 USES "PYGARG" INSTEAD OF "IBEX."

DID YOU KNOW. . .

- When it rains, the ibex does all it can to avoid getting wet.

- The ibex stands on its hind legs to reach leaves in trees.

- The ibex receives help in grooming from the birds called "grackles," which pick parasites from its fur coat.

81

JACKAL

THE JACKAL IS A HOWLER!

Type of animal:
Mammal

Find it in the Bible:
Psalm 63:10

The jackal is a cunning and resourceful animal that belongs to the same family of animals that includes wolves, foxes, coyotes, and domestic dogs. In fact, the jackal looks a little like a coyote and a little like a fox.

The jackal has long, slender legs, a pointed muzzle, and big feet that give it the ability to run very fast—up to 10 miles per hour for an extended period of time. The most common coat is sandy yellow to pale gold with brown-tipped hair.

The common jackal lives in the open deserts and grasslands of Africa, Asia, and southeastern Europe. It lives in a social unit, which usually consists of a family. They work together to defend their territory against enemies—including other jackal families. They spend the day in holes or hidden brush and hunt at night.

Jackals usually hunt alone or in pairs. They are perfectly designed to hunt small mammals, birds, and reptiles. Occasionally they assemble in packs to bring down larger animals, such as antelope. Sometimes they feed from carcasses other predators leave behind after they have eaten their fill.

The jackal is a noisy animal, especially at night. Each family has a distinct howl. It starts as a high-pitched, long, drawn-out cry that is repeated several times. Each time the howl is moved to a higher pitch than before. Then there are several short, loud, yelping barks. Often when one jackal raises the cry, others join in.

Most of the biblical references to jackals connect them with desert ruins. For a city or nation to be made a "den of jackals" is for it to be destroyed (see Jeremiah 9:11, 10:22 NKJV). Farmers and herdsmen found the jackal to be a pest, as it destroyed crops and vineyards and often attacked livestock.

DID YOU KNOW...

- The golden jackal is the largest and most common of all jackal species.

- Jackal family members communicate with each other by screaming yells.

- The jackal can hunt prey four to five times its own body weight.

KATYDID

Type of animal: Insect

Find it in the Bible: Leviticus 11:22 NIV

The katydid is a large, winged insect that is often referred to as the long-horned grasshopper because of the length of its antennae. But the katydid is more closely related to the cricket than the grasshopper. It has long, powerful hind legs, which it uses for jumping. The wings are filmy and extend past the body. It has long threadlike antennae that run above its back and curl under its bottom.

There are about sixty-four hundred known species of katydids living in the world today. Most have two pairs of long wings, but some are wingless. Those with wings are poor flyers. Many do not fly but flutter their wings during long leaps.

The katydid can be heard on a warm summer night as the male courts the female with a song, "Katydid-katydidn't-katydid." The female responds with her own call. To make the musical sound, the insect rubs its forewings, one of which is ridged, together. It sounds much like a violin and bow playing. Each species of katydid has its own distinctive call.

Katydids are usually green, but a few are brown. Some are even pink! The green coloring helps hide them from birds and other predators during the day. They can also match the appearance of their surroundings. The leaf katydid can look like a partially eaten or disfigured leaf. The angle-winged katydid has a flattened, humped back with wings that resemble large leaves.

Most katydids feed on leaves, flowers, bark, and seeds, which makes them pests to commercial farmers. Some katydids, however, feed on other insects, snails, and small reptiles.

The katydid is listed in the Mosaic Law as a clean animal because it is an animal that jumps on the ground.

DID YOU KNOW. . .

- The katydid hears through organs on its legs called "tympana."
- Both male and female katydids can produce sounds when they feel stressed.
- The fork-tailed bush katydid often licks its feet to clean its adhesive pads.

KITE

LOOK! A KITE. . .NO IT'S A BIRD!

Type of animal:
Bird
Find it in the Bible
Leviticus 11:14

The kite is a keen-sighted bird of prey belonging to the same family of birds as the hawk and eagle. It has a small head, short beak, narrow wings, and a forked tail. There are two species of kites—the red kite and the black kite. The difference between these two birds is, obviously, the color, as well as the tail. The red kite's fork is more deeply split than that of its black cousin.

The kite is a graceful flyer with amazing maneuverability. To gain height, the kite flexes its wings and twists its long tail from side to side to use air currents to their fullest. It is capable of fast swoops and twisting dives. In flight the kite flaps once, and then it glides for a long distance before flapping again. While gliding, it tucks its wings behind it to create minimal air resistance so that it seems to float in midair.

The kite is both a predator and a scavenger. It eats mostly small mammals, such as mice, shrews, and young hares and rabbits. It will also occasionally eat reptiles, amphibians, and other birds. This bird is useful as a scavenger because it cleans up dead carcasses left by other predators. The black kite is attracted to fires and smoke, where it swoops down on escaping prey.

MY, WHAT YOU'LL FIND IN A KITE'S NEST!

A kite builds a large, sloppy-looking nest, usually in a fork high in a tree. It is quite a hoarder. It picks up artifacts along its travels and adds them to the nest—anything from cellophane bags to keys. It lines its nest with grass or other vegetation and sometimes sheep's wool.

The Mosaic Law forbade the eating of kites by the Israelites. In the King James Version, the word glede—another name for the kite—is used (see Deuteronomy 14:13).

DID YOU KNOW. . .

- The kite's cry sounds like a high-pitched mewing.

- The kite's tail looks almost like streamers or the tail of a child's kite when the bird is in motion.

- The kite can be a hazard to airplanes taking off at airports.

LAPWING

WHAT'S THAT NOISE I HEAR?

7

he lapwing is a medium-sized inland shore bird with a body mainly of black and white coloring. A
ong, greenish black wispy crest extends from the back of the head, turning up at the end.

The lapwing gets its name from the lapping sound of the wings as it flies. The rounded wings
ave a slow wing beat and give the bird an uneven, flopping flight.

The lapwing is found in wetlands and coastal pastures with short grass. During mating
eason, the male lapwing announces his presence to potential mates by wobbling, zigzagging,
olling, and diving in flight.

The lapwing builds its nest and lays its eggs on the ground in shallow hollows of open meadows.
he nest needs to be close to bare, damp ground where young birds can feed. It also needs to be in
ough or well-planted ground to help hide it from predators. The female lays four eggs, which hatch
n three or four weeks. The chicks are covered in down when they hatch, and the parents quickly lead
hem to places where they can find food.

The lapwing is very protective of its young. When a predator is near, the bird will pretend to have
. broken wing, drawing the predators away from the young birds.

The lapwing has a shrill, catlike cry, "Pee-wit, wit, wit-eeze, wit." The call can be heard along
he shores and meadows, especially during mating season and when the bird defends its young
gainst predators.

The lapwing is listed in the Mosaic Law as an unclean bird, which means the Israelites were not
o eat it. The bird is called a "hoopoe" in some modern Bible translations.

DID YOU KNOW. . .

- Other names for the northern lapwing are "peewit" and "green plover."
- The lapwing's throat is black in the summer and white in winter.
- The lapwing's eggs were once prized and were gathered and sold as food.

LEECH

YUCK! A BLOODSUCKER!

Type of animal:
Annelid
Find it in the Bible
Proverbs 30:15

The leech is an annelid, a type of worm that lives in wet places. It has a long, flattened body that is soft but tough and is usually black or brown. One end contains a head with two to ten eyes and a mouth. The leech's body is made up of thirty-four segments with a large disk-shaped sucker on the last few segments.

There are hundreds of species of leeches. Some live in freshwater, some in saltwater, and some in moist ground. All leeches are carnivorous. Some eat prey such as worms, insects, and snails, which they swallow whole. Other leeches feed on blood from animals and sometimes from humans. These blood eaters have suckers they use to attach themselves to a host (the source of the blood they eat). They use mucus and suction to stay attached to the host, and they squirt an anti-clotting enzyme called "hirudin" into the host's bloodstream. They stay attached until they are full and then fall off to begin digesting their meal.

The leech is equipped with a "crop," which is a type of stomach it uses to store its food. The crop allows the leech to store blood in volumes up to five times its body size.

Many kinds of animals—including several species of fish—like to eat leeches. The leech hides from predators in thick plant growth or mud. If attacked, it tries to swim away fast or go limp and play dead. The leech may also curl into a ball and sink to the bottom of the water.

The leech is mentioned only once in the Bible. Perhaps the writer of Proverbs 30 referred to the leech as having a greedy appetite when he wrote, "The leech has two daughters 'Give! Give!' they cry" (Proverbs 30:15 NIV).

DID YOU KNOW. . .

- The smallest leech is about one-half inch long, and the largest leech is about twelve inches long.
- Some nonsucking leeches can swallow an earthworm whole.
- Most leeches live in the sea, but some live in freshwater and some on land.

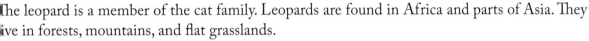

LEOPARD

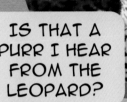

Type of animal:
Mammal

Find it in the Bible:
Jeremiah 13:23

IS THAT A PURR I HEAR FROM THE LEOPARD?

The leopard is a member of the cat family. Leopards are found in Africa and parts of Asia. They live in forests, mountains, and flat grasslands.

The leopard has short legs, a long body, and a large skull. The animal comes in a variety of coat colors, from light buff or yellowish brown to darker shades, even black. The patterned spots, which are called "rosettes," are circular or square depending on the region where the leopard lives. Even the long tail has rosettes. The spots help it hide from other animals and help camouflage it when stalking its prey.

The fully grown leopard stands up to two and a half feet tall at the shoulder and measures three to six feet long. The tail is two to three and a half feet long. Male leopards weigh up to two hundred pounds, but the females are slightly smaller.

The leopard has a keen sense of smell that helps it in hunting for food. It stalks its prey by slinking through the grass or bush. It keeps its head low, legs bent, and belly nearly touching the ground until it is close enough to pounce on the prey. When it does pounce, it bites through the back of the neck, damaging the spinal cord of the prey. Then it strangles the victim.

The leopard's coat is partly made up of patterned spots. . . and no two leopards' spots are exactly the same!

The leopard is not a picky eater. If a deer, antelope, wildebeest, or other large animal can't be found, the leopard will make due with a meal of small animals—even as small as birds or rodents. The cat is a powerful swimmer and is at home in and near the water. It sometimes eats fish or crabs.

The leopard has an amazing method of protecting its food from other animals. Rather than let a hungry lion or other animal steal its meal, the leopard will carry its prey up into the branches of a tree. A leopard's jaws are strong. It can carry animals up to three times its own weight.

The leopard will announce its presence with a raspy cough that sounds like a buzz saw. It also growls and spits with a screaming roar of fury when angry, but it

This leopard is taking a nap in one of its favorite places to be: up a tree!

purrs like a kitten when it is content.

The leopard spends much of its day sleeping in trees, underneath rocks, or in the tall grass. In the evening, it descends from the tree headfirst to hunt until dawn.

The word *leopard* appears several times in the Bible, which means the writers must have been familiar with the cat. Leopards would have lived in biblical lands in the surrounding forests, grasslands, and even deserts. Since leopards are meat-eating animals, herdsmen of sheep, cattle, and goats would have been fearful of them. When the Bible refers to a leopard, it's mostly as a symbol to help teach a lesson.

Jeremiah used the leopard in his preaching. He asked the people, "Can. . .the leopard [change] its spots?" (13:23 NIV). This was to remind them that they had done wrong things for so long that it would be hard for them to change.

Hosea reminded the people of Israel that God was angry with them because they had forgotten Him: "I will come upon them like a lion, like a leopard I will lurk by the path" (Hosea 13:7 NIV).

In another Bible passage, the leopard is used to show what God's kingdom will be like once Christ returns to earth. The prophet Isaiah wrote that wolves will live with lambs, and leopards will lie down to rest with goats. Cows and oxen will eat with bears and lions. All will be at peace with one another (see Isaiah 11:6).

WOW! THERE WILL BE ANIMALS IN HEAVEN!

DID YOU KNOW. . .

- Leopards are solitary animals that like to live and hunt alone.
- Like human fingerprints, no two leopards' markings, spots, or coloring are alike.
- Leopards can run up to 35 miles per hour.
- Leopards are the only "big cats" that carry their prey up a tree.

LEVIATHAN

Type of animal:
Reptile?

Find it in the Bible:
Job 41:1

WHAT A SEA MONSTER!

The leviathan is a mysterious biblical creature, because no animal currently living on earth fits its description. Scholars have debated whether the animal is a crocodile or a whale—or perhaps some type of dinosaur. The facts about the leviathan are written in Job 41:

- The leviathan cannot be caught with a fishhook (vv. 1–2).
- Its mouth has a ring of fierce teeth (v. 14).
- Its back has rows of shields (v. 15).
- Sparks of fire shoot out of its mouth, and its eyes glow like the morning sun (vv. 18–19).
- Smoke comes out of its nostrils like steam (v. 20).
- Its strength is in its neck, and the chest is hard as rock (vv. 22, 24).
- It rises up and causes fear (v. 25).
- It cannot be killed with a spear (v. 26).
- Its underside is sharp and leaves a trail in the mud (v. 30).
- It is a powerful and ferocious creature without fear (v. 33).

Could the leviathan have been a large crocodile? The crocodile has fierce teeth and scales, but an arrow can do much damage to it. Its eyes rise out of the water before the rest of the head, which could fit the description in Job 41:19. The crocodile cannot rise far from the water or ground. The underside of the crocodile is smooth, not sharp, leaving a trail in the mud. The crocodile does not swim deep in the water, stirring it up. No fire shoots from its mouth. Even though many fear the crocodile, this creature does not completely fit the description of the leviathan given in the Bible.

The whale is even less likely to fit the description, even though it can sink deep into the water and surface shooting a stream of water. A spear or harpoon can certainly kill or injure the whale.

Was the leviathan a crocodile or whale, or was it some mythical sea creature—as some scholars think? God's description of the leviathan seems to describe a dinosaur-like, water-living reptile that terrorized the waters during Job's lifetime. The leviathan was among the "real" creatures that Job knew about and that God spoke about as being made along with man.

One sea creature that might match the description of the leviathan is the kronosaurus, an animal from the family of the plesiosaurs. This sea monster was not a true dinosaur (meaning an animal that lived only on land) but a marine reptile. It could reach lengths of thirty feet and had a head six to ten feet long. It had a short, stocky neck with a large head with powerful jaws and a mouthful of sharp teeth. The teeth are believed to have been able to crack the shells of animals such as turtles.

The leviathan could have been any number of creatures—some of which are now extinct. But what exactly it was remains a mystery.

DID YOU KNOW. . .

- The leviathan was the greatest creature in the sea, and nothing on earth was its equal.

- Job 41 includes amazing details about a creature called the "leviathan."

- Scientists have found pieces of turtle shells inside the stomach cavities of a fossilized kronosaurus, proving the power of the jaws and sharp teeth.

This is an artist's drawing of an extinct sea creature called a kronosaurus. Could this be the leviathan mentioned in the Book of Job?

LION

MY, WHAT
BIG TEETH
YOU HAVE!

he lion is the tallest and most powerful of the "big cats." It is covered with yellowish brown
r and has a long tail ending with a tuft of black hair.

You can tell a male and female lion apart just by looking at their physical differences. The
ale has a large, flowing mane that gives him a regal appearance and makes him look bigger,
hich is helpful during confrontations with other male lions. The female, which is called a
ioness," is much smaller than the male. A full-grown male lion usually weighs between 350
nd 550 pounds, while the lioness weighs between 260 and 400 pounds.

Lions live in groups called "prides." There are usually one to four males in a pride, but there
re many lionesses and cubs. A lioness stays in one pride all her life, but a male lion stays for
st a few years. Eventually a younger, stronger male lion will drive it out of the pride. The
ale lions usually stay on the fringes of the pride's area, keeping an eye out for intruders.

The pride normally hunts at night. The lionesses do most of the hunting. Lions have
owerful forelegs, strong jaws, and long canine teeth that help them hunt and kill their prey.

Lions don't
usually do much
during the day. . .
other than lying
around napping
and waiting
until it gets dark
outside.

They prefer to hunt larger animals so the whole pride can eat.

The lion spends much of its time resting and is inactive for about sixteen to twenty hours of the day. Its peak activity is after dusk, with a period of socializing and grooming. The lion communicates by head rubbing—nuzzling its forehead, face, and neck against another lion. This appears to be a form of greeting.

Lions are now found in the wild in sub-Saharan Africa, in parts of Asia, and in northwest India. They used to be found in North Africa, the Middle East, and Western Asia but have disappeared from those areas in recent decades.

During biblical times, lions made their lairs in the forests, mountain caves, and canebrakes on the banks of the Jordan River. The lions were not only a danger to shepherds watching their sheep in the fields, but they often lay along roadsides waiting to attack people.

Several biblical stories mention lions. Here are a few of them:

DANIEL IN THE LIONS' DEN

This is an artist's painting of the prophet Daniel in the lion's den. Even with all those hungry lions around him, Daniel was safe!

In Old Testament times, lions were used as punishment for disobeying the orders of kings. Daniel 6 tells the story of King Darius being tricked into throwing Daniel into a den of lions because he refused to worship the king. But the following morning, Darius ran to the mouth of the den to find that Daniel's God had kept him safe—even though he had just spent the night in a pit filled with hungry lions!

DAVID'S BATTLE WITH A LION

A lion also played a part in the story of David's historic battle with the giant Philistine warrior named Goliath. When David was a young boy, he watched the sheep in his father's fields. He carried a stick to protect his sheep from wild animals. On more than one occasion, he had to kill a lion with the stick when it tried to steal one of his sheep.

Later, as David tried to persuade King Saul to let him fight Goliath, he said to the king, "Your servant has been keeping his father's sheep. When a lion or a bear came and carried off a sheep from the flock, I went after it, struck it and rescued the sheep from its mouth. When it turned on me, I seized it by its hair, struck it and killed it. . . . The Lord who delivered me from the paw of the lion and the paw of the bear will deliver me from the hand of this Philistine"

See 1 Samuel 17:34–35, 37 NIV

OTHER BIBLE PASSAGES THAT MENTION LIONS INCLUDE JUDGES 14; 2 SAMUEL 17:10; PSALM 17:12; AND 1 PETER 5:8.

DID YOU KNOW. . .

- Even though the lion is called "king of the jungle," lions don't actually live in jungles.
- A lion can run as fast as 50 miles per hour.
- A lion's roar can be heard from up to five miles away.
- A large male lion can eat sixty-six pounds of food at one time.
- Male lions are the only members of the cat family with a mane.
- "Lion tamers"—people who train lions to perform in shows—usually have a college education in zoology or veterinary medicine.

93

LIZARD

WOW! LOOK AT THAT DRAGON!

Type of animal:

Reptile

Find it in the Bible

Proverbs 30:28 NIV

The lizard is a long-bodied reptile that lives everywhere in the world except Antarctica. There are nearly thirty-eight hundred known species of lizards. Most lizards have two sets of short legs and long tails. A few species, however, don't have legs and look more like snakes than lizards. Some lizards have short tails. The lizard's skin is covered in scales, which helps protect the animal from injury.

Like other reptiles, the lizard is a cold-blooded animal. That means it cannot control its body temperature like warm-blooded creatures (birds and mammals) can. Because lizards are cold-blooded, most of them live in warm climates. Because lizards are unable to produce their own body heat, they need the sun's heat to warm their bodies. On very hot days, lizards must sometimes find shade, because most of them can't survive if their body temperature goes too high. To escape the scorching midday sun of the desert, lizards burrow below the surface of the sun-baked sand where the temperatures are cooler.

Lizards can be found in almost every color, from black to bright orange to metallic blue to a mixture of colors and patterns. Some species can turn many different colors and patterns according to their emotions and surroundings. Lizards use colors to blend into their surroundings for protection from their enemies. They also rely on body language, using specific postures and movements to protect their territory.

The lizard's tail is one of its most interesting and useful features. For some lizards, the tail almost

This animal looks like a snake, but it's actually a lizard—a California legless lizard. No kidding!

The emerald basilisk is sometimes called the "Jesus lizard" because it can walk on water!

- Some monitor lizards taste the air with their forked tongue to track their prey.

- Lizards range in size from around an inch to more than ten feet long.

- The Komodo dragon is the heaviest lizard, weighing in at up to 330 pounds when it is fully grown.

rves as a fifth leg. It aids in balance and helps those that run pright on their hind legs to attain great speed. One type of zard—the basilisk lizard—uses its hind legs and tail to skim ver water so quickly that it never gets wet! Some lizards ave the ability to wind their tails around tree branches when imbing. And others can scale walls and ceilings of buildings.

The lizard's tail is also important in self-defense. Some zards have sharp, spine-covered tails, which they use as eapons to lash at their enemies. Others can shed their ils when a predator tries to catch and eat them. The vered tail continues to jump around, distracting the nemy while the lizard makes its escape. The lizard then ows a new tail within a few months. When food is arce, the lizard will sometimes eat its own tail!

Most lizards are meat eaters that like to dine on insects nd other prey. They use their small, sharp teeth to grab nd hold the catch while the jaws make a series of quick napping movements over the animal. Many lizards wallow their prey whole.

Most lizards spend their time on land, but some are strong swimmers. or example, the marine iguana spends nearly all its time in the water, here it feeds on saltwater algae. Also, the Nile monitor lizard spends lot of its time in the water, where it feeds on fish, snails, frogs, ocodile eggs, baby crocodiles, snakes, and other foods it can find.

There are several different kinds of lizards mentioned in the Bible. ll of them are listed in the Mosaic Law as unclean.

FIND THE DIFFERENT KINDS OF LIZARDS IN LEVITICUS 11:30.

LOCUST

WOW—AN ARMY OF LOCUSTS!

Type of animal:
Insect

Find it in the Bible
Deuteronomy 28:3

The locust is a kind of grasshopper that gathers in swarms—sometimes huge ones—and travels great distances and causes terrible damage to crops. There are several species of locusts. The desert locust has caused awful damage to crops to the Middle East, Asia, and Africa for centuries. The adult brown locust is about three inches long and has powerful hind legs that help it jump great lengths.

When this powerful jumper is ready to leap, it folds its hind legs up and tucks its feet underneath its body. The legs are held in this position by a special catch inside the knee joint. As the leg muscles contract, the catch on the knee is opened. The leg straightens out with a kick and launches the locust into the air.

Young locusts cannot fly but can hop long distances in search of food. As a locust grows, it sheds its skin. It clings to a twig, and the old skin splits down the back. The locust pulls free, leaving the empty skin. It hops around the ground with millions of other locusts, molting and searching for food. As it grows, it sheds its skin six times. At the final molting of the skin, the locust has fully working wings and can fly well.

Locusts gather together in swarms in search of food. The swarms are sometimes so dense that the sky is darkened. The swarm can strip a field bare of green vegetation in a couple of hours.

According to Mosaic Law, locusts are considered a clean food for the Israelites to eat. The eating of locusts is mentioned in the New Testament—John the Baptist ate locusts and wild honey in the wilderness (see Mark 1:6).

One locust isn't a problem, but when they get together in swarms, look out!

A PLAGUE OF LOCUSTS

The Old Testament book of Exodus tells how a swarm of locusts devastated the nation of Egypt when Pharaoh refused to let the Israelites leave their lives of slavery and travel to their own land.

God had sent Moses to Pharaoh to tell him to free the Israelites, but Pharaoh refused. God had sent seven plagues, but still Pharaoh would not let the Israelites go. So God told Moses, "Go to Pharaoh and tell him that I will send locusts to cover the ground." Again, the stubborn Pharaoh said, "No, I will not let the people go."

So God told Moses to stretch out his staff. When he did so, the wind blew in the swarm of locusts and they covered the ground. They ate everything that was left after the other plagues. They even moved into the Egyptians' houses and ate the food there.

This locust was photographed in 1915, during a locust plague in the Bible lands.

Pharaoh sent for Moses and then told him, "Tell your God to take the locusts away."

Read Exodus 10:18–20 to see what happened.

DID YOU KNOW. . .

- A locust can jump more than forty times its body length.
- A single locust can eat its own weight in grass and leaves each day.
- In 1874 a swarm of locusts estimated to cover 198,000 square miles and numbering 12.5 trillion insects was recorded.
- The desert locust can fly as fast as 20 miles per hour.

LOUSE

I WANT TO SCRATCH WHEN I THINK ABOUT LICE!

Lice (the plural for louse) are tiny wingless insects with short legs, flattened bodies, and antennae on their heads. Lice are no larger than a sesame seed.

There are more than three thousand known species of lice, and they make their homes on the bodies of nearly every bird and mammal known to man. Most of them are scavengers that feed on dead skin and other debris found on their hosts' bodies, but some of them feed on blood and other bodily fluids.

Some lice have hook-shaped claws and six strong legs that cling to the hair of the animals they live on and feed from. They use three slender needlelike mouthparts to pierce the skin. These lice feed on blood several times a day.

Most lice are not dangerous to human health, but they can spread from person to person quickly and can be very annoying. They cannot jump or fly. They are spread through close contact with a person or through shared items such as a hat or hairbrush. Lice attach themselves to hair and snuggle close to the scalp where it is dark and warm. When they get hungry, they crawl down, poke a hole in the skin, and take a sip of blood. The bite usually causes the skin to itch.

Female lice lay eggs on strands of hair. They fasten the eggs in place with a liquid that sets like superhard glue. When the young lice are ready to hatch, the top of the eggs come off and the baby lice squeeze their way out.

Lice are mentioned in the King James Bible in two places. Exodus 8:17 recounts the third Egyptian plague, when God sent lice to Pharaoh and the people of Egypt. In Psalm 105:31, David recounts the story of Moses and the plague of lice. Many newer Bible translations use the word gnats in place of lice.

DID YOU KNOW...

- Lice cannot jump or fly.

- The egg of the louse is called a "nit."

- Some biting lice feed on the feathers and skin of poultry, pigeons, and other birds.

MAGGOT

Type of animal:
Insect (Larvae)

Find it in the Bible:
Exodus 16:20

IT'S HARD TO BELIEVE THESE ARE USEFUL!

Maggots are the larvae of insects, especially those of flies. They are the soft-bodied, legless grubs that are the middle stage in the lives of some insects. Their parents lay their eggs in rotting organic matter—and that's what they feed on!

Although maggots are repulsive, both in looks and in what they eat and where they grow, they are very useful in the medical world. Believe it or not, many doctors use them today to treat flesh wounds that are stubborn to heal. The maggots eat away the damaged tissue, which helps the wound heal.

Maggots are mentioned in the Bible in reference to death (see Isaiah 14:11) and to the low place of humans when compared with God (see Job 25:6).

MANNA-EATING MAGGOTS

After God set the Israelites free from Egyptian bondage and slavery, Moses led them into the wilderness. After their food and water were gone, they began to complain because they were hungry. Moses prayed and asked God to provide food for the people.

God sent the people manna, which was small round flakes, each morning with the dew. His only limitation on eating the manna was, "Gather only what you will need for the day. Don't save any for future days."

The next day, God left manna for the people. Some of the people did not believe God would supply their needs for later days, so they saved more than they needed for the day. The following morning, the saved manna was full of maggots and smelled very bad.

See Exodus 16:11–20

DID YOU KNOW...

- Maggots hatch from eggs within twenty-four hours after the female fly lays them.

- Maggots are usually found near or in garbage, dead animals, and rotting food.

- Some fishermen use maggots as bait.

MOLE

DOES A MOLE HAVE EYES?

Type of animal:
Mammal
Find it in the Bible
Leviticus 11:30 KJV

A mole is an animal that looks like it is closely related to rodents like mice. But moles aren't rodents at all but part of a family of animals known for eating large numbers of insects.

The mole's round body is covered with gray-black fur. It has a short tail, a long snout, and tiny eyes that are hard to see because they are obscured by hair on the animal's face. Moles burrow through soft, sandy soil with their long, sharp front claws. They eat bugs and earthworms that live underground.

The mole's tunnel includes a special underground compartment called a "mole larder," which it uses to store food to eat later. Since the mole's saliva contains a toxin that paralyzes earthworms, it can store the prey for later eating.

Most moles burrow underground. A few species spend part of their lives in water. The star-nosed mole is a good swimmer and forages along the bottom of streams for food. It has water-resistant fur and scaled feet. This mole has a strange-looking circle of twenty-two pink fleshy tentacles at the end of its snout, which it uses to identify food by touch.

Several animals are similar to the mole in appearance and behavior. One is an animal often called a "golden mole," sometimes called a "mole rat." Though it is called a "mole rat," it is not considered a true mole. It is much larger than the true mole, feeds on vegetables, and burrows on a larger scale.

This animal burrowed among the ruins of ancient cities and is found in abundance on the plains of Palestine today. It might be the "mole" mentioned in the Bible. In some Bible translations, the word mole is replaced with the words rat or lizard.

DID YOU KNOW. . .

- The mole can eat three times its body weight in one day.

- The star-nosed mole can detect, catch, and eat food faster than the human eye can follow it.

- Some moles are considered pests because they burrow through the soil, raising molehills and killing plant roots.

MOTH

ype of animal:
nsect

ind it in the Bible:
Matthew 6:19

WHAT ATE A HOLE IN MY SWEATER?

he moth is an insect closely related to the butterfly, but there are several differences between he two. While most butterflies have thin antennae, the moth has feathery antennae. Most utterflies have smooth, slender bodies, while most moths have fatter, furrier bodies. And while ost butterflies tend to be active during the day, most moths are active during the night. These e just a few examples of the differences between moths and butterflies.

The moth uses its antennae, which are also called "feelers" and "smellers," to find food and, hen the time is right, a mate. When a moth lands, it folds its wings against its body or points em out flat from its sides.

The moth's tongue is long and curled up inside itself like a spring. It unrolls the hollow ngue to sip nectar—like sipping soda through a straw.

Some moths are unattractive pests. Their caterpillars, such as those of the hawk moth, do eat damage to plants. The caterpillars of some moths even eat holes in clothing.

Not all moths are pests. Some are helpful to humans. During the night, some moths are active pollinating night-flowering plants. Moths are also a source of food for other animals.

Many moths are very colorful and pretty to look at. The tiger moth uses its bright colors to warn predators of danger. It tastes disgusting and can be slightly poisonous if eaten. It produces a high-frequency sound that jams the sonar system of bats that find moths delicious.

The giant silkworm moth does not have a mouth and cannot eat. All the energy it needs is stored in its body from the food it ate while

Many moths aren't very colorful, but some, like this scarlet tiger moth, are beautiful to look at.

101

a caterpillar. Because of this, the silkworm moth sometimes lives only a day or two.

The male robin moth has huge antennae that he uses to detect a female's scent from a great distance away. After the robin moths mate, the female does not fly far, because she is loaded down with eggs. She usually lays hundreds of eggs on the nearest tree. After a week or so, the larvae hatch and start feeding on the leaves of the trees.

When the moth breaks out of its cocoon, it is wrinkled and wet. It pumps body fluid into its wings until they unfold and dry. Then it is ready to fly.

Job 13:28 makes reference to the destructive habits of the clothes moth. The moth must have been a well-known insect, which in its caterpillar state was destructive. This destructive power used to illustrate the result of sin in Psalm 39:11.

STORE UP YOUR TREASURES IN HEAVEN

Jesus used moths as part of a lesson He taught His followers on the mountainside. He had been teaching His followers about many important things. He warned them not to store up treasures on earth where moths would destroy them and thieves would break in and steal them. Jesus told the followers to store treasures in heaven instead, where moths could not reach them.

See Matthew 6:19–20

Having learned this important lesson that Jesus had taught, the apostle James later warned rich people not to be so concerned with their wealth. He told them that their wealth would rot and moths would eat their clothes.

See James 5:2

DID YOU KNOW...

- The hawk moth can fly up to 30 miles per hour.

- The Atlas moth is the largest known moth, with a wingspan of up to twelve inches.

- The larva of the hawk moth, called a "hornworm," is an eating machine, chomping up both poisonous and nonpoisonous (to people) plants.

MOUNTAIN SHEEP

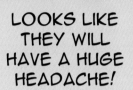

Type of animal:
Mammal

Find it in the Bible:
Deuteronomy 14:5

LOOKS LIKE THEY WILL HAVE A HUGE HEADACHE!

A mountain sheep is one and a half times bigger than its domesticated cousin. Its coat coloring is from light tan to chocolate brown, and it has a white rump. Under the sheep's outer wool are "guard hairs"—long, coarse hairs that shed water and snow. Under the "guard hair" is a layer of wool that traps the animal's body heat to help keep it warm. When a mountain sheep sleeps, it folds its legs under its body to help keep them warm, too.

The mountain sheep's amber yellow eyes can spot things a mile away. This sharp eyesight is the animal's best defense against predators. The mountain sheep also has sharp senses of smell and hearing.

Male mountain sheep are called "rams" and females are called "ewes." The rams have thick, curved horns that can weigh up to thirty pounds. The horns sometimes form a complete circle on each side of the head. The ewes have smaller horns that are not quite as curved.

Mountain sheep eat only plants. They graze on grasses and shrubs, but they will seek minerals at natural salt licks. In winter, when the snow covers the ground, the mountain

Mountain sheep aren't afraid of heights. In fact, they're built to live in places that most other animals wouldn't dare go!

sheep sometimes dig in the snow with their hooves to find grass and plants to eat.

These sheep live high in the mountains, where they find protection from predators. Most predators are not sure-footed enough to chase them along the narrow mountain trails. Only the cougar hunts in the high mountains. The parents must protect the young sheep, called "lambs," from golden eagles, which can swoop down and snatch them up.

The mountain sheep can leap a 150-foot cliff and land safely. Their hooves have a hard, sharp outer edge that cuts into the earth, gravel, and ice. The center of their hooves is made of spongy material that provides traction. The split hooves can pinch and hold on to rocks. Two smaller claws high up on the foot serve as brakes if they begin to slip. Even sheep as young a two or three weeks old can jump and climb in rugged, dangerous mountain areas.

Mountain sheep live in "bands" of ten to one hundred animals. During mating season, horn clashing between the males takes place. Two rams will circle each other at a distance of about thirty feet apart. They approach one another and rear up on their hind legs and charge head down at full speed. Their heads crash together, making a cracking sound that can be heard from a mile away. They keep the horn clashing up until one of the rams wears down or gives up. Sometimes the clashing lasts for several days and nights.

Mountain sheep were listed in Mosaic Law as animals the Israelites could eat. Not only were the mountain sheep hunted for meat, but also their horns were used as trumpets (Joshua 6:4) and as oil containers (1 Samuel 16:1).

DID YOU KNOW. . .

- The mountain sheep never sheds its horns, which only grow larger every year.

- The mountain sheep sheds its thick winter coat in spring and grows a new coat by the following winter.

- The mountain sheep can run as fast as 35 miles per hour.

- A mountain sheep can leap seven feet into the air.

Type of animal:

Mammal

Find it in the Bible:

Leviticus 11:29 KJV

MOUSE

> MICE WILL EAT ANYTHING THAT DOESN'T EAT THEM FIRST!

7

Mice are small rodents with pointed noses, whiskers, beady black eyes, round ears, and long hairless tails. Five toes on each of their four feet help them grip when climbing. Mice use their sharp teeth for gnawing on food and, as a last resort, biting predators.

Mice run, walk, and stand on all four legs. But when they eat, they stand on their hind legs, using their tails for support.

Mice have a long list of enemies. Many different kinds of birds, reptiles, mammals, and even fish love having fresh mouse for dinner. Their only defenses are to blend into their surroundings or to run to safety. Since they are small, mice can fit into tight places predators can't reach.

In the wild, mice live near open fields and forests, but they commonly make their homes in houses and other manmade structures They dig burrows near food supplies because they like to eat fifteen to twenty times per day. They make paths connecting their homes to food sources. They also store food in several hiding places.

Mice are considered pests. They eat seed stored by people, damage crops, and carry disease. The best known of the mice species—the common house mouse—has been domesticated and is a popular pet, but it is also a pest in the home.

The Mosaic Law lists mice as unclean and forbids eating them. As a guilt offering for stealing the ark of the covenant, the Philistines were advised to send "five golden mice" to the Israelites when they returned the ark to them (1 Samuel 6:4–5).

> SOME BIBLE TRANSLATIONS USE THE WORD RATS INSTEAD OF MICE.

DID YOU KNOW. . .

- Mice stay in one place all their lives unless food runs out or their homes get too hot or cold.

- Instead of sleeping at night, mice take several short naps in the day.

- Mice rely on their size, speed, and cleverness to survive.

- It is believed that the domestication of cats was first done with the purpose of controlling mouse and rat populations.

105

MULE

STUBBORN AS A MULE, REALLY?

Type of animal:
Mammal

Find it in the Bible
1 Kings 1:33

A mule is the offspring of a male donkey and a female horse. It has a short, thick head, long ears, thin limbs, small, narrow hooves, and a short mane like a donkey. But it has the height, shape of neck, coat, and teeth of a horse. It comes in all sizes, shapes, and characteristics of both donkey and horse.

The mule is more patient, sure-footed, hardy, and longer-lived than a horse. It is less stubborn, faster, and more intelligent than a donkey. The mule may appear to be stubborn, but it is actually just a cautious animal that does not want to be put in a dangerous position.

Every mule has a unique bray. Its sound is similar to the bray of a donkey but also similar to the "whinnying" of a horse. It often sounds like this: "Whinee-aw-ah-aw."

The mule's hooves are harder than a horse's, and they work well in clay soil. For that reason, farmers for centuries have plowed their clay-soiled fields using mules.

Like many "hybrids" (animals that result from crossbreeding), all male mules and most female mules are infertile, meaning they can't produce offspring.

Since the Mosaic Law outlawed crossbreeding of animals, the Israelites of biblical times imported mules. They were used as war animals, for riding, and for carrying burdens. They were also used for moving heavy burdens, being better than a horse, donkey, or camel.

It is likely that only kings and the wealthy rode on mules in Old Testament times. David chose a mule to symbolize royalty for Solomon's coronation as the king (see 1 Kings 1:33).

DID YOU KNOW. . .?

- The average mule can carry about two hundred pounds.
- A mule is a very curious animal.
- The mule is sure-footed and can live and work in much rougher country than a horse can.

OSPREY

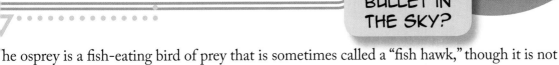

Type of animal:
Bird

Find it in the Bible:
Leviticus 11:13 NIV

> IS THAT A SPEEDING BULLET IN THE SKY?

The osprey is a fish-eating bird of prey that is sometimes called a "fish hawk," though it is not really a hawk. This bird can be found on every continent in the world except Antarctica.

The osprey differs from other birds of prey, as its toes are equal in length. The outer toe is reversible, allowing it to grasp prey with two toes curved forward and two curved backward. The talons are also rounded rather than grooved.

The osprey, with its narrow wings edged with four long, fingerlike feathers and a short fifth feather, circles the water searching for food. When the bird's sharp eyes spot a fish, it plunges toward the water with its wings bent back and legs bent. It reaches its legs forward as it nears the water. The feet break the surface of the water as the osprey snatches up the fish. It takes the fish back to its perch to eat it. An osprey's diet consists of about 99 percent fish, but if fish are not available, it will catch and eat small mammals, amphibians, or reptiles.

The male osprey displays courtship for a mate by soaring high and diving with fantastic spins. Sometimes the male will carry a fish as a gift to the female. The two build a bulky nest of sticks and seaweed in a tree or rocky cliff. Ospreys sometimes build their nests on top of telephone poles and other manmade structures. The female lays two to four white eggs then begins incubating them. The male feeds the female while she sits on the eggs.

The osprey is listed in the Bible as an unclean bird. It is still found around the lakes and the coasts of the Mediterranean Sea.

> THE IDENTITY OF THE BIRD IN THE BIBLE IS QUESTIONABLE. SOME TRANSLATIONS CALL IT A "BLACK VULTURE," SOME A "BLACK EAGLE," AND OTHERS A "BUZZARD."

DID YOU KNOW. . .

- The osprey is sometimes called a "fish hawk," as it is closely related to a hawk and feeds on fish.

- The osprey has a black "eye patch" that runs back to its neckline.

- The osprey flies with its wings held in an M-shape.

- A pair of ospreys will mate for life.

107

OSSIFRAGE

THAT'S A STRANGE NAME FOR A BIRD!

Type of animal:
Bird

Find it in the Bible:
Deuteronomy 14:12 KJ

The bird referred to as the ossifrage in the King James Bible has been identified by some Bible scholars as what is now called the "bearded vulture." This bird gets its name from the black "beard" of feathers on its chin. This bearded vulture has large, narrow wings with a span of about nine feet and a long, wedge-shaped tail. It also has deep red eyes, which are not found in any other vulture species.

The underparts of the bearded vulture are usually colored deep orange. It acquires this color by rubbing against rocks containing iron oxides.

The bearded vulture is found in high mountainous areas above tree lines. A pair of these birds builds an enormous nest in a rocky crevice where the female deposits one or two pinkish or yellowish eggs. After they hatch, the young spend 106 to 130 days in the nest before venturing out to fly on their own.

The bearded vulture does very little hunting for food. Instead, it waits until other vultures have eaten the fleshy parts of the carrion and then picks the bones to eat the marrow, which makes up about 90 percent of its diet. Sometimes the bird carries large bones high into the sky then drops them. When they fall on the rocks below, they crack open, making it easier for the bearded vulture to get to the marrow. Occasionally the bearded vulture does the same thing to a tortoise, which it also likes to eat.

WHAT A WAY TO EAT!

The ossifrage is mentioned in Mosaic Law in a list of birds that are unclean. Eating carrion makes it unclean. The Hebrew word for ossifrage means to "crush" or "break," making it a fitting name for the bearded vulture!

DID YOU KNOW...

- Unlike most other vulture species, the ossifrage does not have a bald head.

- The ossifrage can live up to forty years in captivity.

- It takes a young ossifrage up to two years to develop red eyes.

OSTRICH

Type of animal:
Bird

Find it in the Bible:
Job 39:13

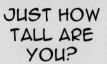

JUST HOW TALL ARE YOU?

he ostrich is the largest of all birds. It has wings, but it can't fly. Ostriches stand between six and
ine feet tall and weigh between 140 and 290 pounds when they are fully grown. The males have
lack and white plumage, while the females are brownish gray. The ostrich has a long neck and a
mall head with large eyes. The eyelids have long lashes made up of fringes of hairlike feathers. The
strich has very good eyesight and can see danger from a long way off.

Although the ostrich cannot fly, it can walk or run fast enough to escape
ny of its enemies. It has two long, enormously powerful legs with large,
ooflike, two-toed feet that allow it to run as fast as 45 miles per hour,
naking it the fastest runner of any bird. An ostrich can cover up to sixteen
eet (the size of a family car) in one step.

JOB 39:13–18 TELLS THE CHARACTERISTICS OF THE OSTRICH.

Ostriches use their speed to outrun predators, but if they have to, they
an defend themselves by kicking their enemies with their powerful legs. The
emale ostrich lays the biggest eggs of any known animal—up to three pounds
ach. She lays her eggs in depressions in the sand and incubates them during the day. The male
strich sits on them at night.

Ostriches are now found in the wild only in Africa, but they once lived in the Middle East.
he Bible lists the ostrich as unclean, meaning the Israelites were not to eat it. This could be
ecause of its eating habits. It has been known to swallow substances such as iron, stones, and,
n modern times, bullets.

DID YOU KNOW. . .

- The ostrich can go without water several days but enjoys taking a bath.
- A wild ostrich can live to be thirty to thirty-four years old.
- Contrary to what many people believe, ostriches don't really bury their heads in the sand.
- Ostriches are now raised on farms and are prized for their plumes, their meat, and their hides.

OWL

WHAT BIG EYES YOU HAVE!

Type of animal:
Bird
Find it in the Bible:
Psalm 102:6

The owl is a bird of prey that usually lives and hunts alone. Most often hunting during the nighttime, it flies on nearly silent wings and swoops down on the small creatures it eats, grabbing them with its huge talons. Some owls can carry off prey larger than themselves.

Depending on the species, an owl feeds on anything from insects to mammals as large as rabbits. Most owls swallow their prey whole. The parts of the meal they can't digest—fur, bones scales, and feathers—they cough up in the form of pellets.

An owl has big eyes, a short, hooked bill, and a round face. It cannot move its eyes but turns its head to look to the side. Owls have excellent vision and depth perception, but most owls don't see well close up.

There are more than a hundred species of owls. The largest is the great eagle owl, which grows to twenty-eight inches long and has a wingspan of more than six feet. The smallest is the elf owl, which grows to only five inches long. Not all owls make the hoot sound. Different species make different sounds.

How an owl mates and nests depends on the species. Some owls nest in trees, sometimes using the old nests of other birds. Some nest on the ground in marshy or open grasslands. Some owls even nest underground in the abandoned burrows of other animals.

The Bible mentions several different kinds of owls, all of which are listed in the Mosaic Law as unclean. Some of the species were common in Palestine and were often found inhabiting the ruins of cities. Deuteronomy 14:15–17 (NIV) lists a number of owl species—the horned owl, the screech owl, the little owl, the great owl, the white owl, and the desert owl.

DID YOU KNOW. . .

- The owl's soft wing feathers allow it to fly silently.
- The owl has a keen sense of sight and hearing.
- The female owl is much larger than the male owl.
- Though owls tend to be solitary birds, a group of owls is called a "parliament."

ype of animal:

Mammal

ind it in the Bible:

euteronomy 22:10

OX

TWELVE YOKE OF OXEN EQUALS TWENTY-FOUR!

he ox is a heavy-bodied bovine (in the same family of animals as cattle) animal with short gs and sliced hooves. It chews cud, meaning it consumes its food then brings it back up om its four-part stomach to chew it again later. The ox n't really an individual species of animal. It is commonly adult bull that has been neutered and trained to perform rtain tasks for its owners.

In Old Testament times, oxen were extremely valuable as work nimals. Farmers depended on their oxen for all the ordinary perations on the farm. Oxen were commonly used for plowing, r treading out corn, for pulling, and for transporting people and aterials. They were also sometimes eaten.

Oxen were usually yoked in pairs to do the work their owners eeded them to do. A specially designed wooden yoke was stened around the neck of each pair. The oxen were trained to respond to the ox driver's signals. Sometimes, depending on the work, oxen worked in teams of as many as twenty animals.

Oxen were also used in several methods of threshing. They were driven over the grain lying on the threshing floor. Their hooves did the work of threshing. Another method was having the oxen pull a threshing board over the grain while e thresher stood on the board.

God gave the Jews a strict code of ws regarding the treatment of their xen. The oxen that threshed the corn ere not to be muzzled. They (along ith their masters) were also to be rested n the Sabbath.

READ OW ELISHA LOWED WITH WELVE YOKE OF OXEN IN 1 KINGS 19:19.

OTHER BIBLE VERSES THAT MENTION OXEN ARE EXODUS 23:12; NUMBERS 7:3; AND DEUTERONOMY 25:4.

DID YOU KNOW...

- The word oxen, as the Hebrews used it, meant both male and female.

- Both male and female oxen have horns.

- Oxen can pull harder and longer than horses, which make them better with heavier loads.

- A person who drives a team of oxen is sometimes referred to as a "teamster."

PARTRIDGE

THAT BIRD MUST BE TIRED AFTER LAYING THAT MANY EGGS!

Type of animal:
Bird

Find it in the Bible
1 Samuel 26:20

The partridge is a medium-sized game bird belonging to the pheasant family. It has a plump body with a deep chest, a feathered tail, round wings, and a short, thick bill. It is smaller than most pheasants but larger than most quail. It is ten to fourteen inches long and weighs less than a pound.

Partridges are found in the wild in Europe, Asia, Africa, and the Middle East, which includes biblical lands. They live in groups called "coveys," which consist of a male, a female, the young, plus a few other birds. The partridge feeds on grain, seeds, and insects.

During the mating season, a pair of partridges builds a shallow, grass-lined nest on the ground, where tall grass conceals them from predators. The female is a very nervous mom when sitting on the eggs. Sometimes, if she is disturbed, she will abandon the nest.

To avoid predators, the partridge uses its deep chest to propel it quickly across the ground to safety. The partridge prefers to run rather than fly, but if pursued it will fly a short distance.

The Bible refers to the partridge as the hunting bird upon the mountain. The Greek partridge somewhat resembles the chukar or rock partridge but is much larger. It has a brown back with black and white bars on the sides, a black outlined head with a white throat, and red legs and bill. It lives in the hill country of Judea. Its ringing call, "Kar-wit, kar-wit," is heard in early morning.

DID YOU KNOW. . .

- The gray partridge lays the largest cluster of eggs of any bird—nineteen to twenty eggs.
- Most species of partridges do not migrate but stay in the area where they were raised.
- The partridge is sometimes associated with the grouse, bobwhite, and quail.
- Two species—the chukar and the gray partridge—have been successfully introduced to North America.

PEACOCK

Type of animal:
Bird

Find it in the Bible:
1 Kings 10:22 KJV

BEAUTIFUL, PROUD—BUT A BIT TOO NOISY!

The peacock is one of the most beautiful birds in the world. The peacock—the male of a bird called "peafowl"—spreads his long, beautiful tail, which is colored with markings of gold, green, and purple. He has a blue-green or blue head, neck, and breast. The female, called a "peahen," is mostly brown with a shiny green neck and shorter tail feathers.

The peacock, which is native to India and is India's national bird, spends much time grooming his tail. Every feather must be in place. The peacock uses his tail to show off to the peahen. He begins his ritual with a few shivers and shakes. Then there is a sound like rustling silk as the layers of feathers seem to open and float upward. The shivers get stronger, and soon the whole tail is spread. He prances back and forth in front of the peahen with his tail spread and his head held high. He announces his act with an ear-splitting yell: "EEEooo...LOOoww...EEEonn...LEEow!"

The peacock often spends the night in a tree, on a fence, or on a rooftop. He doesn't fly very well, and sometimes he lands on the ground in the morning with an undignified *kwwammp*! He eats insects, plants, and even small reptiles. The peacock really likes eating small cobras, which are dangerous to humans. He uses his long legs and sharp spurs to protect himself against enemies.

The peacock is mentioned in the Old Testament. When King Solomon's fleet of ships arrived in Jerusalem, they brought many valuable items, including peacocks. Solomon kept peacocks around the royal palace because they showed his wealth and majesty.

SOME BIBLE TRANSLATIONS REPLACE "PEACOCK" WITH "OSTRICH." OTHER KING JAMES BIBLE VERSES MENTIONING THE PEACOCK ARE 2 CHRONICLES 9:21 AND JOB 39:13.

DID YOU KNOW...

- When you combine the length of his tail and his wingspread, the peacock is one of the largest flying birds in the world.

- The peacock is from the same family of birds as the pheasant.

- The peacock's tail can be more than six feet long.

- A group of peafowl is called a "pride" and usually includes one peacock and several peahens.

PELICAN

THAT'S QUITE A FISHING NET YOU HAVE THERE!

Type of animal:
Bird

Find it in the Bible
Psalm 102:6 KJV

The pelican is a large seabird. It has a huge bill with a huge pouch that hangs from the lower part of the bill. There are more than six species of pelicans. They live on coastlines and also near lakes and rivers. They live and travel in flocks and breed in groups called "colonies."

The pelican's pouch is made of skin and stretches to hold up to three gallons of fish and water. Most pelicans feed by scooping up water and fish in the shallows then lifting their heads and forcing the water out. All that's left in the pouch is the pelican's food, which it swallows whole.

Like other species of pelicans, the brown pelican lives in large colonies. But it is the only pelican species that feeds by diving. It flies over the water from as high as sixty or seventy feet in the air, looking for fish to eat. When it spots its prey, it dives under the water, making a big splash.

Special air sacs under the brown pelican's skin and bones hold pockets of air. The air sacs cushion the impact as the pelican hits the water. Then all the air in the body makes it bounce back to the surface like a cork.

The pelican's nest is made of twigs and seaweed and is usually close to water. Both parents feed and care for the young. The parents feed the youngsters on partly digested fish. When the mother or father pelican arrives at the nest, the babies put their heads into the adult's throat and feed.

Pelicans are found in Palestine. In the King James Bible, Leviticus 11:18 and Deuteronomy 14:17 forbid the people of Israel to eat the pelican's meat. In Psalm 102, David compares his sad mood to a pelican, probably because the pelican looks sad as it rests its bill on its breast.

DID YOU KNOW. . .

- A group of pelicans is called a "pod."

- A pelican must eat four pounds of fish a day to survive.

- A pelican never carries water or food around in its beak.

Type of animal:
Mammal

Find it in the Bible:
Mark 5:11

PIG

THAT PIG IS TAKING A BATH—IN MUD!

The pig has short legs, a thick, heavy body, and a small tail that is either curly or straight. It has a thick, coarse coat of brown or gray fur. The pig has four toes on each foot with the two large toes in the middle used for walking. The pig's snout, which it uses to root around in the dirt for food, includes very sensitive smell organs.

Pigs are omnivores, meaning they eat meat, plants, and other foods. The pig eats plants, bugs, and insects, along with grains the farmer feeds it.

The pig is most active early in the morning and just before dark. It spends much of the time sleeping, only waking to eat and drink. When a pig sleeps alone, it usually lies on one side with its legs sticking straight out.

A pig is a social animal. It enjoys close contact with other pigs and with other animals. Pigs often cuddle together when they sleep so they can keep warm. They grunt and squeal to communicate with one another.

A female pig is called a "sow" and a male pig a "boar." Baby pigs are called "piglets" and can walk soon after they are born. Before they are ready to eat solid food, the piglets feed on milk

When it's time for lunch, baby pigs go where they know they can get something to eat. . . straight to mom!

from their mother. The sow grunts when she calls the piglets to tell them it is time to eat. The sow can feed twelve piglets at once. If she has more than twelve babies (which she sometimes does), the extras are given to another sow to feed.

Wild pigs are called "wild boars." They are smaller than farm pigs and have more hair. They also have tusks for digging and fighting other boars. They can destroy a farmer's crop with their digging for food.

A pig is used for meat as well as for leather. Pigskin can be used to make purses, wallets, and gloves. Some paintbrushes are made from pig bristles. Some baseball gloves are stuffed with hair from pigs.

The pigs of the Bible were probably wild pigs, which are still common in Palestine. While the Canaanite pagans kept herds of pigs, the Mosaic Law listed them as unclean animals and forbade the eating of their meat. Even those who tended the pigs were not allowed to enter the temple.

Many ancient people ate pigs and used them as animal sacrifices to their idols. The pigs were pests to farmers because they dug up crops in the fields.

THE PRODIGAL SON

One of Jesus' most famous stories (called "parables") mentioned pigs.

When the religious leaders of Jesus' time—the scribes and Pharisees—complained that He spent time with "sinful" people, Jesus told the parable of the prodigal son. It was the story of a young man who wanted to leave home so badly that he asked for his inheritance before his father died. The man gave his son the money, and the boy ran off to party. He had lots of friends, until the money ran out—and when a famine struck the land, the only job he could find was feeding pigs.

The Jews hated pigs, since they were an "unclean" animal according to Moses' law. When the boy realized what a mistake he'd made—that he was wishing to eat the pigs' food when his father's servants were better fed—he decided to go home and ask his father if he could serve him as a slave.

But the father was so thrilled to see his boy coming home, he threw a party. The point of the story? God loves it when sinners "come home."

See the whole story in Luke 15:11-32.

JESUS AND THE DEMON-POSSESSED MEN

Pigs played an important part in one account of Jesus healing two demon-possessed men He and His disciples encountered one day. They were passing through the area called the Gadarenes when they met two men coming from the tombs where they lived. The men were controlled by evil spirits and were so wild that people stayed away from the area because they were afraid.

The men shouted, "Son of God, what do You want with us? Have You come to punish us?"

Not very far from the men was a herd of pigs that were eating. "If You drive us out of the men, send us into the herd of pigs," the demons begged Jesus.

Jesus said to the demons, "Go!"

The demons came out of the men and went into the pigs. Then the entire herd ran down the steep cliff into the lake and drowned.

You can read this whole story
in Matthew 8:28–34.

A herd of pigs played an important part in the story of Jesus healing a man who was tormented by evil spirits.

DID YOU KNOW. . .

- Pigs are also called "hogs" or "swine."
- A pig likes to wallow in wet mud to keep it cool on a hot day.
- Pigs are very intelligent and learn quickly.
- An adult pig can weigh as much as a piano!
- A pot-bellied pig makes a good pet.

PIGEON

WOULDN'T IT BE FUN TO SEND A MESSAGE BY A PIGEON?

Type of animal:
Bird

Find it in the Bible
Leviticus 5:7

The pigeon is a plump bird with a small head, a short, slender bill, and large wings. With its strong wing muscles, the bird can make low wing landings. A soft swelling that plays an important role in breathing is found on the pigeon's beak.

Most pigeons have a blue-gray body with two dark wing bars. There are twenty-eight pigeon color types with a variety of patterns. Pigeons come in an assortment of sizes, too. The smallest, a ground pigeon, is the size of a sparrow. The crowned pigeon, the largest species of pigeon, is nearly the size of a turkey—four to eight pounds.

Pigeons mate for life and can nest at any time of the year—though the peak times are in the spring and summer. They build their nests from sticks and other debris. In the wild, they nest in cliffs, but they will nest on building or bridge ledges that resemble cliffs. Some pigeons prefer to build on the flat ground.

The female pigeon lays one or two eggs, and both male and female care for the young, which are called "squabs." Both parents produce and feed their young "crop milk," sometimes called "pigeon milk." They keep the crop milk in a saclike food storage chamber that shoots outward from the bottom of the esophagus.

Pigeons are a common sight in nearly every city around the world.

Pigeons were the first animals to carry messages for people. The Romans trained pigeons to carry news of battles back and forth to the generals. During World War I and World War II, pigeons saved many lives by carrying messages across enemy lines. Pigeons are easily trained and seem to have a built-in "homing" device within them that allows them to return home after flying long distances.

In the Bible, pigeons are named as birds used for sacrificial offerings. Sometimes the dove and pigeon, which are closely related, were interchanged with each other. They were used for both burnt offerings and sin offerings. They were also used as an offering for a healed leper. Pigeons were one of the least expensive animal offerings. People who could not afford to sacrifice a sheep or goat would offer two pigeons, which they could buy in the temple courts.

GOD'S COVENANT WITH ABRAM

One day God and Abram were talking together. "Look at the stars, Abram," said God. "Count them if you can. That is how many descendants you will have."

Abram believed God and built an altar. God told him to bring a heifer, a goat, and a ram, along with a dove and a young pigeon. Abram brought all of those animals and put them on the altar. Then God made a covenant, or agreement, with Abram.

You can read the whole story in Genesis 15.

DID YOU KNOW. . .

- The pigeon is one of the strongest fliers of any bird.

- The pigeon sucks up water using its beak like a straw.

- Some pigeons can fly 40 to 50 miles per hour and can fly as far as six hundred miles in one day.

- Many pigeons have received military awards and medals for their service during wartime.

119

PORCUPINE

BALLOONS WOULDN'T BE A GOOD IDEA AT A PORCUPINE PARTY!

Type of animal:
Mammal

Find it in the Bible:
Isaiah 34:11 ASV

The porcupine is a large rodent (in the same family as mice and rats) with a short, rounded body. There are about twenty-four species of porcupines around the world. They are found in Asia, Africa, America, and Europe.

The porcupine's best-known feature is the coat of sharp spines or quills that defend it from predators. The porcupine has soft hair, but the hair on its back, side, and tail is mixed with the quills.

The porcupine keeps its quills flat against its body—at least until the animal is threatened. Then the quills spring upward. The quills are hollow and have sharp tips with overlapping scales or barbs. The barbs make the quills difficult—and very painful!—to remove once they are stuck in a predator's skin.

Contrary to what many people believe, the porcupine can't throw its quills at attackers. The quills are released when a predator comes in contact with them. They may also be dropped when a porcupine shakes its body. The porcupine grows new quills to replace the lost ones.

Porcupines are plant-eating animals that like to dine on bark and twigs. They are fond of hemlock, fir, pine, maple, beech, birch, oak, elm, cherry, and willow. Some porcupines can climb trees and have been known to do damage to trees by stripping them of their bark. They will also eat fruit and springtime buds.

Porcupines also crave salt. They will eat just about anything that has salt on it, including plywood, tool handles, shoes, clothes, and tires. The porcupine is attracted to roads where rock salt has been used to melt ice and snow.

Porcupines mate in the fall and give birth in the spring. Baby porcupines are called "porcupettes." The mother porcupine gives birth to between one and three babies. Porcupines are born with spines, but they are soft and flexible.

The porcupine lives in a wide range of places—forests, grasslands, deserts, and rocky hillsides. Palestine still has porcupines, as it did during biblical times.

DID YOU KNOW. . .

- A group of porcupines is called a "prickle."

- A porcupine may have thirty thousand or more quills.

- The African crested porcupine's quills are nearly a foot long.

ype of animal:

rd

nd it in the Bible:

umbers 11:31

WHO
IS BOB
WHITE?

he quail, which is a member of the pheasant family, is a small, plump ground bird that lives the tall grasses and brushy borders of the plains and farmlands. It has sturdy legs, head umage curling forward, and a curved bill. Its feathers are usually brown, speckled with hite, black, or chestnut. These colors blend with the grassy surroundings, camouflaging the rd from predators. The quail is mostly a seedeater but will also eat insects and other small eatures, some of which are harmful to farmers' crops.

The quail spends most of its life on the ground, running and zigzagging through the grass. he quail is not a strong flying bird, but when necessary, it can fly short distances.

The female quail, which is called a "hen," is rger and stronger than the male, which is called "rooster." She does the nest building. She builds er nest in a scratched hollow of the ground, sually concealing it under shrubs, logs, or rocks nd lining it with leaves or grass. In the spring, ne lays eggs, which the male helps incubate. Both male and male quail care for the young.

One of the daily activities of the quail family is ne dust bath. They select an area where the ground soft. Using their underbellies, the quail burrow ownward for one or two inches. Then they wiggle bout, flapping their wings and ruffling feathers, ausing dust to fly into the air.

The male quail is designated as the family uard. He perches on a high place to keep watch ver the clan. When he sees danger approaching, e uses a variety of calls to warn his family. The est-known quail call is "bob-white, bob-bob-hite," which comes from a species called the bobwhite."

The quail the people of Israel gathered in the wilderness probably looked more like this bird—the common quail—than the bobwhite quail we see in America.

The quails mentioned in the Old Testament differ from the "bobwhite" quails we see in America today. Besides being migratory, which American quails are not, the quails of the Bible are shorter, stockier, and spotted brown in color. The bill is smooth and the legs are spurred.

The quail is mentioned in the Bible only in connection with God's provision of food for Israel in the wilderness. It is probable that these quail, which visited the Hebrew camp, were a migrating flock. Enormous numbers of quail migrate north during the spring. When the birds stop to rest, they can be easily caught—even by hand. It has also been noted that quail migrate at night. In God's timing, the birds came to provide for the needs of His people. (You can read the whole story in Exodus 16.)

Like chickens, quails provide food for humans in two ways—by their meat and by their eggs, considered a delicacy in many countries.

DID YOU KNOW. . .

- Young quails leave the nest as soon as they have hatched but stay with their parents during the first summer.
- The quail (or family of quail) lives individually but forms flocks to migrate.
- Because the quail's wings are short, it must beat them rapidly to fly.
- The quail is considered a game bird and is hunted by humans.

RABBIT & HARE

Type of animal:
Mammal

Find it in the Bible:
Deuteronomy 14:7

WHAT BIG TEETH YOU HAVE!

A rabbit is a furry animal with long ears, short tail, and powerful hind legs for speedy running. It has big front teeth, which never stop growing. It prefers to nibble on grass and other plants at dusk or during the night. The rabbit lives in meadows, woods, thickets, and grasslands in many parts of the world. Some rabbit species are also found in deserts and wetlands.

The rabbit is a sociable animal that lives in family groups. Several rabbits dig a group of connected burrows called a "warren." There are many separate entrances into the burrow and some quick escape routes.

The hare, sometimes called "jackrabbit," is often mistaken for the common rabbit, simply because the two animals look so much alike. It is closely related to the rabbit, but there are several differences between the two animals.

First, the hare is larger and heavier than the rabbit, and it has longer ears. It also has black markings on its legs. The hare has powerful back legs that enable it to jump high and fast.

Unlike the rabbit, the hare is not a social animal but lives and moves around individually. Instead of living in underground burrows, the hare lives in the open countryside. When it needs shelter or rest, it goes to a shallow trench in the long grass called a "form," which it makes itself. Because of its color, the hare is well camouflaged as long as it stays still.

Hares put on an amazing display during mating season. They chase each other, leap in the air, and "box" each other. Scientists used to believe that the two "sparring partners" were male hares (called "jacks") fighting for the right to mate with certain females (called "jills"). But recently it has been observed that it is usually a female rabbit hitting a male. That could be because she is not quite ready to mate, but it could

Hares and rabbits are closely related, but there are differences between the two animals. How does this hare look different from the rabbits pictured above?

also be to test the male to see how much he really wants to mate.

Unlike baby rabbits, which are born blind, naked, and helpless, baby hares are born with a full coat of fur and with their eyes open.

There are also several similarities between the rabbit and the hare. They are both fond of all green growing things and have earned a reputation for doing damage to gardens and field crops. In the winter, both feed on the bark of trees and shrubs, which damages the plants.

The rabbit and hare are both well equipped to detect enemies. Their long ears are very sensitive. When the animal is at ease, the ears lie quietly along its back. But at the slightest sound, the ears stand upright, waving backward and forward, as they try to locate the danger.

The nose of both animals is also very sensitive. As they try to pick up scent, the nostrils twitch and the head moves up and down. The two eyes also see in every direction, even scanning overhead. The tail is used to alert others of a predator.

The rabbit and hare are hunted by many different predators and are constantly on guard against them. When threatened, they will freeze and observe. The five toes on the forefeet and four on the hind feet give the animal the ability to make a fast getaway.

The Bible lists rabbits and hares among the unclean even though the animal does not have a split hoof.

The rabbit and hare were valued by hunters for their meat and fur. They were pests to the farmer because they often damaged crops.

IN SEVERAL BIBLE TRANSLATIONS, SUCH AS THE KING JAMES VERSION, THE WORD HARE IS USED INSTEAD OF RABBIT.

DID YOU KNOW. . .

- A rabbit can run 25 miles per hour and jump ten feet.
- Some hares can run up to 45 miles per hour and jump fifteen feet.
- The rabbit or hare can see behind itself without moving its head.
- The rabbit and hare can hop, jump, leap, and zigzag every which way as they streak forward, with lightning-fast movements.

Type of animal:

Bird

Find it in the Bible:

Luke 12:24

RAVEN

LOOK OUT FOR THE THIEF!

The raven is a member of the crow family, but it is much larger than the common crow, sometimes weighing more than three pounds. It has black, glistening plumage, a large beak, shaggy throat, and a wedge-shaped tail. The raven is known for its intelligence and for its remarkable ability to solve problems.

Though the raven is omnivorous—meaning it eats plants and meat alike—its diet varies with its location. In some areas, it is mainly a scavenger that feeds on food waste and animal carcasses. In other areas, it feeds on insects and other bugs, small amphibians and reptiles, and small mammals and birds. It becomes a pest to a farmer when it eats grains, berries, and fruit and damages crops.

The raven's wide and complex vocabulary consists of much cawing and croaking. It has an alarm call, a chase call, a flight call, and many others. The raven even has a few nonvocal sounds, such as the whistling of wings and the snapping of the beak.

Young ravens travel in flocks, but later they mate for life and defend their territory against other pairs of ravens. Only when they have obtained a territory are a pair of ravens ready to build a nest. The nest is a deep bowl made of large sticks and twigs and bound with an inner layer of roots, mud, and bark. It is lined with soft material such as deer fur. The nest is built in a high tree or in a cliff ledge.

Raven chicks look out of their nest to see who's coming. Is it mom with something to eat?

125

RAVEN

OTHER BIBLE VERSES THAT MENTION THE RAVEN ARE DEUTERONOMY 14:14; PSALM 147:9; AND ISAIAH 34:11.

Ravens are very protective of their nests and are even known to drop stones on predators that get too close.

The raven is listed in the Mosaic Law as an unclean bird. But it is also listed as an example of God's care for His people. The raven was the first bird Noah sent out from the ark following the flood (see Genesis 8:1–7). Noah may have chosen the raven for several reasons. It can fly without rest for long spans of time. Also, it makes its home in the rocky crags and would probably scout out mountain peaks emerging from the flooded earth. Finally, the raven is a resourceful bird with a remarkable memory.

In another biblical account, ravens served as symbols of God's love for His servant Elijah. After Elijah told the wicked King Ahab that it would not rain, God sent him to the brook. God told Elijah, "You will drink from the brook, and I will send ravens to feed you."

Elijah did what God told him to do. He drank from the brook, and the ravens brought him bread and meat in the evening (see 1 Kings 17:1–5).

DID YOU KNOW...

- A raven calls other ravens to share its food bonanza, usually a carcass.

- A raven steals shiny objects, such as pebbles, metal, and golf balls.

- Ravens like to have fun and have been seen sliding down snowbanks.

- A raven may hide surplus food out of sight from other ravens.

- In the 1840s, Edgar Allen Poe wrote a famous poem called "The Raven." In the poem, a bird taps on the window of a man who's sad about a girl he loved. The raven makes him even sadder by saying "Nevermore, nevermore"!

ROOSTER

Type of animal:
Bird

Find it in the Bible:
John 13:38

DOES A ROOSTER REALLY DANCE?

The rooster, which is an adult male chicken, has a solid body, strong feet, spurs on his legs, and a short pointed beak. Unlike the hen, he has long, flowing tail feathers and shiny hackles (long, pointed feathers) on his neck and back. The large, fleshy, red growth on his head is called a "comb," and the flap of red skin hanging under his beak is called a "waddle."

The rooster is well known for its crowing, especially just before dawn. In past years, before there were alarm clocks, farmers relied on roosters to wake them in the mornings. Roosters also crow at other times of the day.

There are many theories about why roosters crow. One of them is that the rooster is sounding an alarm of danger or disturbance to the other chickens. Another is that the rooster is simply "announcing his presence" to potential predators or other roosters. Some believe the crowing is part of the rooster's mating ritual.

At night, the rooster (as well as the hen) perches on a roost to sleep. The rooster guards the hens while they are nesting. The rooster is territorial and will attack other roosters who try to enter his territory. During the day, the rooster sits on a high perch and guards the flock.

Two colorful roosters fighting to settle their differences over territory

127

ROOSTER

PETER DENIES JESUS. . . BEFORE THE ROOSTER CROWS

At the Last Supper, hours before the crucifixion, Jesus told His disciples that He would be leaving them soon and they would not be able to follow. Peter told Jesus, "I will lay my life down for You."

Jesus answered Peter, "Before the rooster crows, you will disown Me three time."

When Jesus said that Peter would deny Him "before the rooster crows," He may have meant before dawn. Some roosters crowed at other hours. The Roman soldiers used one late-night crowing as a signal to change the guards.

Later, when the soldiers took Jesus, Peter followed him but had to wait outside in the courtyard. A servant girl asked Peter, "Are you one of the disciples?"

Peter answered, "No, I am not."

As Peter stood warming himself by the fire, he was asked again. "Are you one of the disciples?"

Again Peter answered, "No, I am not."

Then one of the servants who had been with the soldiers who arrested Jesus asked Peter, "Didn't I see you with Jesus?"

Just as Peter denied it, a rooster began to crow. The crowing reminded Peter of what Jesus had said. He was sorry for his actions and words

See Matthew 26:31–35, 69–75

When Peter heard the rooster crow, he remembered what Jesus had told him.

THE ROOSTER IS POLITE AND HAS GOOD MANNERS.

Like the hen, the rooster scratches and claws the ground looking for food—grains, worms, insects, and other kinds. When the rooster finds food, he calls other chickens to enjoy a meal with him. He does this by clucking with a high-pitched call, as well as by picking up and dropping the food.

When the rooster wants to court a hen, he will drag [on]e wing on the ground while circling around her. This [co]urting ritual "dance" lets the hen know he wants to [ma]te with her.

The Bible says little about roosters, but the people of [Isr]ael were apparently familiar with them. In the Old [Te]stament, King Solomon compares the king parading [be]fore the people to a "strutting rooster" (Proverbs [30]:31 NIV).

DID YOU KNOW. . .

- The male chicken is called a "rooster," but males less than a year old are called "cockerels."

- Some breeds of rooster crow almost constantly, while others crow only a few times during the day.

- A rooster begins to crow when he is only four months old.

- A bold, red rooster makes up the flag of Wallonia, a French-speaking region in the south of Belgium. The flag was designed in 1913.

SCORPION

WATCH OUT FOR THAT SHARP STINGER!

Type of animal:	Find it in the Bibl⟨
Arachnid	Deuteronomy 8:1⟨

The scorpion is a small crawling animal that looks a little like a flat lobster. It has a thick body with a "head" consisting of eyes, mouthparts, claws (or pincers), and four pairs of leg⟨ There are two eyes on top of the head and two to five pairs along the front corners of the head. The narrow, segmented tail ends with a poisonous stinger. The scorpion moves along in a threatening stance with its tail in the air. It feeds on spiders and insects, crushing the⟨ in its pincers or injecting venom to kill or paralyze them.

Though it might be easy to mistake the scorpion for some kind of insect, it is actually what is called an "arachnid." Arachnids are a lot like insects in some ways. They both hav⟨ shells around their bodies called "exoskeletons." But arachnids have eight legs instead of six. Also, the scorpion's body is divided into two parts, while the bodies of insects are divided into three parts.

Scorpions also have a pair of organs called "pectines," which they use to sense the

Some scorpion moms take care of their babies until they are mature enough to take care of themselves.

...mallest movements around them. This helps them ...hunting down prey and in sensing the presence of ...otential predators.

...During the daytime heat, the scorpion spends its ...me in dry, dark places, such as under rocks and logs or ...the ruins of buildings. It comes out at night to hunt ...d eat.

...During courtship, the scorpion pair performs a ...ance." The male grasps the female's claws and leads ...r around. He even gives her a kiss! After the young ...orpions are born, the female carries them on her back ...til they molt once.

...The inhabitants of biblical lands feared scorpions. ...ey were a danger when Moses led the children of ...rael through the hot, rocky wilderness. God told the ...ophet Ezekiel not to be afraid of his enemies, whom ...e referred to as "scorpions" (Ezekiel 2:6).

...Jesus taught of the perfect love of God ...hen He pointed out that a ...od earthly father would ...ever give his child a ...orpion instead of an ...g. His point was that ...en the best fathers are ...perfect but still do good ...ings for their children. ...nd if an imperfect man ...es good things for his ...ildren, how much ...ore will God do ...od things for His ...ildren? (See Luke ...:12)

DID YOU KNOW...

- The scorpion's sting is seldom fatal but can be very painful.

- There are about two thousand different species of scorpions.

- Most scorpions are about two or three inches long, but the emperor scorpion, which is found in Africa, can grow up to eight inches long.

- The scorpion's thick body helps protect it from predators.

SHEEP

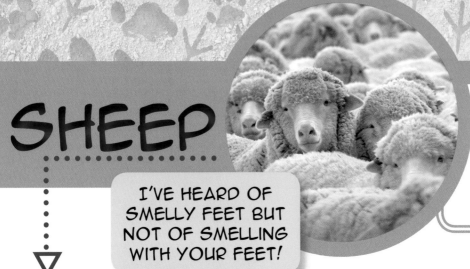

Type of animal:
Mammal

Find it in the Bibl
John 10:3

Sheep have always been important to humans—from biblical times all the way to the present. For many centuries, people have raised sheep for their meat, milk, and wool. Shee fleece is sheared and sent to a factory to be cleaned and spun into wool. Special cheeses and yogurts are made from sheep's milk.

A sheep's thick coat—also called its "fleece"—may be long and curly or short and smooth. It keeps the sheep warm in the winter but is shed in the summer. Most sheep's coats are white, but some are black or dark brown.

The sheep has a good sense of hearing and can be very sensitive to noise. It also has an excellent sense of vision. The sheep can see behind itself without turning its head. It has scent glands in front of its eyes and on its feet.

The sheep's hooves are divided into two toes with scent glands between the toes. Some scientists think the sheep can smell its way back to the flock if lost.

A sheep's mouth is made for grazing on short grass. It bites off grass between its bottom front teeth and upper pad and swallows it. The sheep is a ruminant, meaning an animal that chews the cud. Like other ruminants, sheep have stomachs made up of four chambers, each of which has special functions in the digestion of the sheep food. The cud chewing allows the shee to graze more quickly in the morning and chew later. When grazing, the sheep lowers its head, leaving it expose to predators.

Male sheep are called "rams." Many

Two little lambs snuggling up to their mother for warmth and security.

A shepherd working in traditional clothing in Israel. In some parts of the world, people still make their living working as shepherds.

ms have at least one pair of horns. The horns curve outward on the sides of the head. The rns are used to protect the female sheep and to fight off other rams. Some female sheep ve horns, too, but they are smaller than a ram's horns.

The female sheep is called a "ewe." She usually gives birth to twins. The baby sheep are lled "lambs." The lamb can walk within an hour of birth. Sheep make a high-pitched ise called "bleating." A lamb can identify its mother by her bleat.

As the day turns to night, the sheep gather together to sleep. They find a sheltered area d lie down with their backs to the wind.

In biblical times, sheep wool was spun and woven into warm cloaks and tunics. Tents re made from sheepskins. Rams' horns were used as trumpets (Joshua 6:4) and as oil ntainers (1 Samuel 16:1).

Sheep skins were used in the construction of the tabernacle. Ram skins were dyed red d used as a covering for the tabernacle (see Exodus 25:5). Sheep were also important

animals for temple sacrifices. They were also used as sacrifices at altars built by people wh
worshiped God. Abel was the first keeper of sheep and brought his firstborn from his floc
as an offering to God. Abram made an altar and sacrificed a ram, among other animals,
when God made His covenant with him (Genesis 15:9).

The sheep raised and kept during biblical times were hardy animals that were well-suit
to the rough hill pasture. Shepherds often protected flocks of sheep from wild animals an
lead them to fresh grazing land and watering places.
King David was a shepherd when he was a boy.
He protected the sheep from bears and lions (see
1 Samuel 17:34–37).

THE NEW INTERNATIONAL VERSION MENTIONS SHEEP 205 TIMES, RAMS 101 TIMES, AND LAMBS 103 TIMES.

Having a lot of sheep
was a sign of wealth
in biblical times.
God blessed
Abraham with
many sheep.
He also blessed
Solomon, who
gave 120,000 sheep
at the dedication
of the temple (see
2 Chronicles 7:5).

The Bible contains hundreds of
references to sheep. Jesus made reference to sheep
when He taught His followers during His time on
earth. He told the parable (story) of the lost sheep.
In this story, the shepherd left the ninety-nine
sheep still in his flock to go look for one lost sheep.
Jesus told this story to teach people about the love
of God for His people (You can read the whole
story in Luke 15:1–7.)

Jesus also called Himself the "Good Shepherd"
who knows His sheep, and His sheep know Him.
Jesus cares for us, His sheep (John 10:1–18)!

DID YOU KNOW. . .

- A group of sheep is called a "flock."

- Sheep are social animals and prefer being together in a flock.

- Sheep's wool is the most widely used of any animal.

- A shepherd, sometimes with the help of a sheepdog, takes care of the sheep.

- There are about 150 yards of wool yarn inside a baseball.

ype of animal:

eptile

ind it in the Bible:

Leviticus 11:30 NIV

SKINK

LOOK AT THAT BLUE TONGUE!

THAT'S WHEN STICKING OUT YOUR TONGUE IS PERMITTED!

he skink is part of a family of more than one thousand different kinds of lizards. Most skinks are irly small with cone-shaped heads and very long tails—usually as long as their bodies. The skink oks like other lizards but has no distinct neck and has small legs. Several species have
 limbs at all and look more like snakes than lizards.

Most skinks are carnivores (meat eaters) that like to dine on insects, rthworms, snails, slugs, other lizards, and small rodents.

The skink, like many other lizards, can shed its tail and grow a new one. a predator takes hold of the tail, the skink twitches a muscle and the il snaps off. The tail wiggles and keeps the predator busy while the skink capes.

The blue-tongued skink is colored to blend in with its surroundings, which eps predators from finding it. But when the male wants to attract a mate or to ighten off a rival or enemy, he opens his mouth and sticks out his bright blue tongue.

Most skinks burrow under rocks or logs. Those species that live in the hot climate swim through the nd where it is cooler than above ground.

The skink is listed in Mosaic Law with several other lizards that are unclean and not to be eaten. ome Bible translations call the animal a "snail" (King James Version) or a "sand lizard" (New Revised tandard Version).

DID YOU KNOW. . .

- The largest skink can grow to thirty inches long, but most of them are around eight inches long.
- Most skinks are striped, but a few are spotted or one color.
- The skink sends out a foul-smelling musk to keep enemies away.

SNAIL

WHERE'S THAT SLIME COMING FROM?

Type of animal:

Mollusk

Find it in the Bibl

Leviticus 11:30 KJV

Snails are mollusks that have coiled shells on their backs when they are fully grown. Most snai live in freshwater or saltwater, but there are also many species of land snails. Land snails have thinner shells than the aquatic snails. As snails grow, so do their shells.

The snail's body is made up of two parts. The main part is attached to the inside of the shell. It contains the snail's vital organs. The mantle, a layer of tissue, covers the internal organs. It extends outward in flaps that reach to the edge of the shell.

The soft part of the body that comes out of the shell is mainly muscle. The snail uses this part of its body, which is called the "foot," to move about. The snail's body produces thick, slimy mucus that helps it move along on its muscular foot. The mucus also helps keep the snail safe from injury when it moves over sharp objects.

The snail breaks up its food using a hook called a "radula." In a quiet setting, some land snail can be heard "crunching" their food.

The snail has two eyes on the end of flexible tentacles. Below the eyes, there are two tentacle that aid in smelling food.

The snail is listed in the Mosaic Law as an unclean animal. In Psalm 58:8, the psalmist refer to the slimy track left by the snail, which seemed to be wasting itself away.

DID YOU KNOW. . .

- The snail can withdraw into the shell and close a doorlike structure for protection from predators.
- Some snails have lungs and some have gills.
- The world's biggest snail, the Australian trumpet, a marine species, can grow up to thirty inches in length and weigh as much as forty pounds.

SNAKE

VENOMOUS MEANS POISONOUS!

akes are long-bodied, meat-eating reptiles that don't have legs. Snakes are found in every
ntinent of the world except Antarctica. Many islands around the world don't have snakes living
them.

The snake's body is covered with scales, which help it move on the ground. Snakes also have
ates on their bellies that work the same way as a bulldozer track. The muscles attached to ribs
ive the plates into the ground and move the snake forward. Contrary to what many people
ink, the snake's scales are smooth and satiny, not slimy.

There are many thousands of snake species, and most of them are not venomous. Venomous
akes have long, hollow fangs that are folded back against the roof of the mouth when not in
e. When the snake strikes, the fangs unfold and shoot directly forward and stab the victim and
ject it with venom. The venom either kills or paralyzes the prey. The venom of some snakes can
deadly to people.

Venomous snakes come in a variety
sizes and colors. The different colors
lp to camouflage the snake for better
ncealment in hunting and for protection.
naller venomous snakes eat smaller
imals like insects and frogs while larger
akes eat fish, birds, mice, rabbits, and
her larger prey.

Snakes have limited detailed vision at a
stance, but they see movements around
em immediately. Their "hearing" is limited
ground vibrations that travel through
e jawbone to the brain. The snake's sense
touch is sharp. Smell is the snake's most
owerful sense. It smells through its nasal
ssages and through its flickering tongue,
hich picks up airborne particles. These

Venomous snakes like this rattlesnake
have fangs they use to inject venom.
Notice the drops of venom on the tips of
its fangs.

137

particles are passed through special organs in the mouth alerting the snake to anything near.

Different species of venomous snakes live in different habitats. Some live in wet places along riverbanks and in woodlands. Some live in deserts and some live in the mountains. Like other reptiles, the snake is a cold-blooded animal and will hide away in a burrow or other places on ver hot or very cold days.

Different words for "snake"—such as venomous snake, adder, asp, and viper—appear several times in the Bible. At least thirty-three different species have been found in Palestine. In the desert regions of Egypt, vipers, adders, and asps are very common. When the Bible refers to snakes or venomous snakes, we cannot be certain which type is mentioned unless the kind of snake is specifically named.

There are several passages in the Bible in which snakes play a key role. Here are a few of them

A VIPER BITES PAUL

A viper is the master predator of the snake world. It has facial pits between the eye and nostril. These pits help the viper locate warm-blooded prey, especially at night. The viper can "feel" the heat of an animal and will strike warm targets. That was the kind of snake the apostle Paul once encountered.

Paul was on board a ship that was taking him over the Mediterranean Sea to speak to the high ruler in Rome. Suddenly, a storm came up. Before the ship could reach land, it was dashed against the rocks and broke apart. All the crew and passengers made it safely to land.

They found themselves on an island called Malta. It was cold and rainy, so the islanders made a fire so the crew and passengers could warm themselves. When Paul picked up some sticks to throw on the fire, a viper came out of the bundle and fastened itself on Paul's hand. He brushed the snake into the fire. The islanders thought Paul would die, but God took care of him.

A horned bush viper—a snake very much like the one that bit the apostle Paul's hand at Malta.

You can read the whole story in Acts 28.

A STICK BECOMES A SNAKE

God told Moses to go to Egypt to lead the Hebrew people out of slavery. Moses was afraid the people wouldn't listen to him, so God gave Moses a sign. He told him to throw his shepherd's staff on the ground. When he did, it became a snake. Moses ran from the snake at first, but God told him to pick it up by its tail. When he did, it became a staff again.

You can read the whole story in Exodus 4:1–7.

THE SERPENT ON THE POLE

Moses had led the Israelites out of Egypt. They were in the desert on the way to the Promised Land when they started to complain to God and to Moses. They cried, "Why have you brought us to the desert to die? We have no bread or water. We don't like the food God gave us."

God sent venomous snakes to bite the ungrateful people, and some of them died. The people came to Moses and said, "We have sinned against you and God. Ask God to take away the snakes."

So Moses prayed for the people. God told him to make a bronze snake and put it on a pole. When the people who had been bitten looked at the bronze snake on the pole, they lived.

See Numbers 21:4–9. Other Bible verses that mention snakes are Job 20:16; Proverbs 23:32; Isaiah 59:5; Mark 16:18; and 1 Corinthians 10:9.

DID YOU KNOW. . .

- Most snakes don't hunt but wait for prey to come to them.
- The average speed of a snake is less than 2 miles per hour.
- Snakes sleep with their eyes open because they have no eyelids.
- Horned viper snakes have structures to keep sand out of their eyes and protect them from the sun.
- A side-winding adder buries itself in the sand to escape the hot sun.

139

SPARROW

SUCH A TROUBLESOME BIRD TO BE SO SMALL!

Type of animal: Bird

Find it in the Bible Matthew 10:29

The sparrow is a small, plump, brown gray bird with a short tail and a stubby, powerful beak. The short, pointed beak is ideal for seed cracking. The sparrow is a seedeater but will also consume small insects. It is part of a large group of birds called "perching birds." Its legs and toes are designed for perching on branches and other places where the bird chirps and twitters.

There are about 140 different species of sparrows, and they come in many different color patterns. Sparrows are flocking birds that gather by the thousands and take over feeding and roosting areas. They are sometimes aggressive and will force out other birds and take over their territories.

The sparrow is an intelligent bird that roosts in noisy flocks on branches of trees and bushes, under eaves of houses, and in attic vents. It can be troublesome to people when it nests in such places as gutters, drainpipes, and chimneys, causing water damage and even fires.

Sparrows are found in great numbers in Palestine and are of very little value to people. The Eurasian tree sparrow is very common throughout Europe and Asia and may be seen on Mount Olivet (also called the Mount of Olives) in Jerusalem.

In Matthew 10:29–31, Jesus used the sparrow to teach His followers how much God loves all His creatures—especially humans. If God cares for and feeds even the smallest birds, such as the sparrow, Jesus taught, how much more will He care for people?

OTHER BIBLE VERSES THAT MENTION SPARROWS ARE PSALM 84:3; PROVERBS 26:2; AND LUKE 12:6-7.

DID YOU KNOW. . .

- Because they are so often found in urban areas, the sparrow is considered one of the most familiar wild bi to humans.

- The house sparrow originally lived Europ and much of Asia, bu it has followed huma all over the world an is now the most wide distributed bird on planet Earth.

- The American tree sparrow has a large crop (neck pouch) in which it can store up to one thousand seeds.

SPIDER

Type of animal:
Arachnid

Find it in the Bible:
Job 8:14

YUCK! A SPIDER THAT SUCKS UP GUTS!

he spider is a member of the "arachnid" family. It differs from insects, which have six legs and three dy parts. Spiders have eight legs and only two body parts.

There are more than forty thousand known species of spiders living today. They are found ywhere in the world warm enough to support life. They come in different sizes and colors. Some e fuzzy, some smooth. Some spiders are poisonous, but some are not. Only about a dozen species spiders are considered dangerous to humans.

Even though spiders have four pairs of eyes, they cannot see very well. They use tiny slits in their gs to sense vibrations. They also use chemical sensors to pick up taste and smell.

Nearly all spiders are predators that eat insects and other small animals. Some even eat small ptiles and birds! Many spiders build webs to catch their prey, but some hunt for their food. Those at build webs are called "orb web spiders." The spider uses its sticky web to trap its food.

When an unsuspecting insect or other bug gets caught in the web, the spider rushes over and raps its victim in silk, turning it around and around. Then the spider pokes its fangs into its meal d injects poison that turns the prey's insides into a liquid. Once the spider has cked all the liquid out of the victim, all that is left is a shell of the animal.

There are many species of spiders living in Palestine. Some spin webs, but me dig bottomless cells and make doors in them, and some chase their prey the ground.

OTHER BIBLE VERSES THAT MENTION SPIDERS ARE PROVERBS 30:28 (KJV) AND ISAIAH 59:5.

DID YOU KNOW. . .

- The world's largest spider, the Goliath bird-eating spider, can grow to as large as twelve inches long.
- If a spider loses a leg, it can grow a new one.
- Some species of jumping spiders can leap up to seventy times their own body length.
- The young of some spiders feed on plant nectar.

STORK

I GUESS THE STORK REALLY DOES BRING BABIES.

Type of animal:

Bird

Find it in the Bible

Leviticus 11:19

The stork is a large, long-legged, long-necked wading bird. It is one of the most eye-catching of the wading birds, sometimes standing nearly four feet high. The stork is heavily built with broad, rounded wings. It is a strong flier that extends its neck and trails its legs behind when it is in the air. The adult stork makes no vocal noise. The only sound it makes comes from the clattering of its bill.

Storks build huge nests of sticks on cliffs, in trees, or even atop occupied houses. Some stork nests are as big as six feet wide and three feet deep. The female stork lays two or three eggs in the nest. Both male and female storks take turns incubating the eggs. Baby storks are naked when they are first born but later become covered with feathers. They remain in the nest after hatching. Both parents care for them.

The stork usually wades in shallow pools and marshes in search of food. Most storks eat fish, clams, frogs, insects, earthworms, and small birds and mammals that live in and around the water.

The stork is listed in the Mosaic Law as an unclean bird. Jeremiah 8:7 says that every year the stork knows when to migrate. Storks always stop in Palestine during their migrations. Both the black stork and the white stork are common in Palestine.

OTHER BIBLE VERSES THAT MENTION THE STORK ARE DEUTERONOMY 14:18 AND PSALM 104:17.

DID YOU KNOW. . .

- While resting, the stork holds its long beak pointed downward.

- The stork's plumage is slate gray and white.

- The stork is punctual in returning to the same nesting area at the same time every year.

- The marabou stork has a wingspan of up to ten and a half feet, tying it with the Andean condor for the widest wingspan of all land birds.

SWALLOW

Type of animal:
Bird

Find it in the Bible:
Psalm 84:3

DOESN'T THAT SWALLOW EVER LAND?

e swallow is one of many members of a group of birds called "perching birds." It has a slim blue
ck body, short red brown neck, and pointed wings. It has a deeply forked tail that is uses for
ering as it soars and twists in flight. It needs plenty of air room to make all of its maneuvers. It
kes use of strong wings to migrate long distances.

Because it has short legs, the swallow can only hop around clumsily on the ground. It spends
st of its life either perching or flying in the air. The swallow is an excellent flier that scoops up
ects such as flies and mosquitoes that hover in the air. It even drinks in flight by snatching up
n water in its lower beak.

Some species of swallows nest in colonies. A pair of swallows, male and female, returns to the
ne nest site each year. The birds work together to build a new nest or repair the old one. Some
ecies mix dirt and saliva together to build their nests. They create a hollow ball of mud with a
ge, where the female lays her eggs.

The swallow migrates to Palestine from March until winter. In biblical times, it made its nest
the temple eaves and was often seen with the common sparrow. It was sometimes confused
th the swift or thrush, which some Bible translations use instead of the word swallow.

DID YOU KNOW. . .

- The names swallow and martin are used interchangeably, and there seems to be no difference between them.
- The arrival of the first swallow is sometimes seen as a sign that summer is near.
- The swallow spends most of the day in the air, but at night the family gathers together in a warm nest.
- One colony of barn swallows in Nigeria included 1.5 million individual birds.

143

SWAN

WHAT A MAGNIFICENT, GRACEFUL BIRD!

Type of animal:
Bird
Find it in the Bibl
Leviticus 11:18 KJV

The swan is a large water bird from the same family as geese and ducks. It has a boat-shaped body and webbed feet, which makes it a good swimmer. The swan's wide wingspan makes it a strong flie Because it has difficulty taking off, it must paddle across the water surface with its feet as it flaps it wings to build up speed for takeoff.

Most swans have white feathers with a black beak and feet. To keep the feathers waterproof, the swan smears oil from a gland near the tail onto the feathers with its beak.

The swan lives near shallow water. It feeds on land and in the water. It eats mostly roots and shoots of plants that grow in the water, but it will eat small numbers of water animals.

When the swan feeds in the water, it uses its long neck to reach to the bottom of ponds and rive in search of food. This is called "upending" or "dabbling," a funny-looking scene in which the swan's tail and backside stick out of the water while its head is submerged. When the swan feeds on land, it waddles along the water's edge to graze on grass and plants. It sometimes swallows small pebbles or sand to help it digest its food.

A pair of swans mates for many years—sometimes for life. The pair builds a nest of sticks on raised ground or on the water. Sometimes the nest is nine to twelve feet across and three feet deep. This helps keeps the baby swans safe from the water and from predators. Male swans help in incubating the eggs.

Some swan species are migratory, meaning they travel to warmer areas during the winter. A group of swans can migrate as far as one thousand miles, flying in a V formation. They fly as fast as 50 miles per hour—up to 70 miles per hour with a strong tailwind.

The Mosaic Law calls the swan an unclean bird. In biblical times, the bird lived along the banks of the Mediterranean.

DID YOU KNOW...

- The female swan is called a "pen" and the male is called a "cob."

- Once a year the swan loses its feathers and grows a new set.

- Some species of swan carry their young (calle "cygnets") on their ba to keep them warm an safe.

SWIFT

ype of animal:

Bird

ind it in the Bible:

eremiah 8:7

THAT BIRD IS GOING DOWN THE CHIMNEY!

he swift is a soft brown-colored bird similar in shape and size to the swallow, but it is unrelated the swallow. The swift has a slender body and long, pointed wings with a wide span. It needs enty of room between its shoulders and the ground to flap its wings when taking off.

Some of the birds have notched or forked tails. Some have short tails that make steering vkward. The bird must beat one wing more strongly than the other to change directions. The vift performs many loops and dips in the sky.

The swift has short legs and has difficulty walking. Because of this, it spends most of its life in e air. Swifts are among the fastest fliers of all birds, reaching air speeds of up to 70 miles per our. They use their speed to catch insects to eat in the air.

There are several species of swifts, and they range in size from the pygmy swiftlet (three to four ches long) to the purple needletail (up to ten inches long).

The edible-nest swift lives in colonies of caves. It builds its nest of saliva and sticks it to the roof d walls of caves. It uses a kind of natural radar called "echolocation" to find its way in the dark ves.

The white-collared swift nests in vertical cliffs behind waterfalls. It flies in and out through the aterfall to get to its nest.

The prophet Jeremiah mentioned the swift, along with other birds, when he wrote about a time f migration. Some Bible translations use the word swallow instead of swift in the verse.

DID YOU KNOW. . .

- The swift is an expert flier and one of the fastest flying birds.
- The swift flies long distances at great heights when it migrates.
- The chimney swift gets its name because it likes to build its nest in chimneys.

145

TURTLE
(OR TORTOISE)

DOES A TURTLE EVER GO FISHING?

Type of animal:
Reptile

Find it in the Bible
Leviticus 11:29 KJV

The turtle is a slow-moving reptile with a hard shell that serves sort of like a personal roof. It is the only reptile with a shell, and it protects the animal from heat and from predators.

A turtle's shell can be gray, brown, green, or a mixture of colors, depending on the species. The turtle has sprawling legs with short feet or flippers, depending on the species. It has good eyesight and seems to be sensitive to red. The turtle's ears are flat against the head with skin stretched over the opening.

The turtle has no teeth but uses its hard beak for tearing food apart and grinding it. The tongue is used for moving the food around in its mouth.

There are many kinds and sizes of turtles. Some turtles live on land only, and some live in the ocean. Still others spend part of their time in water and part on dry land. A tortoise is a type of turtle that lives its whole life on land.

The leatherback sea turtle can measure eight feet in length and weigh more than fifteen hundred pounds. The tiny freshwater turtle grows to about four inches long.

What a turtle eats depends on the species. Some turtles eat mostly vegetation, while others are meat eaters. Some eat both plants and meat.

The alligator snapping turtle has an extra tonguelike attachment in its mouth that looks like a worm. It opens its mouth and wiggles its tongue like a fishing lure. The fish thinks it is a worm and moves in to try to eat it. Then— snap!—the turtle has caught a fish for dinner!

The musk turtle, also known as stinkpot, produces a smelly liquid called "musk" to protect itself against predators.

The turtle, which is called a "tortoise" in Leviticus 11:29, is among the unclean animals. The New International Version calls it a "lizard."

DID YOU KNOW. . .

- Most turtles can go days, even weeks, without eating.

- All turtles, even those that live in the ocean, lay their eggs on land.

- Some sea turtles can swim up to 20 miles per hour and travel thousands of miles to return to their nesting sites each year.

VULTURE

Type of animal:
Bird

Find it in the Bible:
Deuteronomy 14:13

SUCH AN UGLY BIRD!

e vulture is a large scavenger bird with an enormous wingspan, short tail, and sharp talons. en though the vulture's talons are strong, the bird does not use them to kill prey. That's cause it eats carrion—animals that are already dead. It uses its slightly hooked beak to tear e flesh of animal carcasses.

Many vulture species have long, naked necks. That allows the bird to reach deep inside rcasses without collecting flesh or blood on its feathers. After eating, the vulture sometimes nds with its wings spread to dry its wings and warm its body. This helps bake off bacteria at smeared on the body while it was feeding.

The vulture has keen eyesight that can detect food miles away by watching other birds in the y. It also finds food by flying low to the ground to pick up the smell of dead animals.

The vulture's powerful wings allow it to fly long distances at high altitudes in search of food. hen it finds a warm pocket of air, it holds its wings motionless. The warm air carries the lture as it soars in circles in the sky, sometimes for hours at a time.

According to the Mosaic Law, the vulture is an unclean bird and not to be eaten. Some Bible anslations replace the word vulture with "buzzard," "eagle," or "kite."

DID YOU KNOW. . .

- A group of vultures is called a "wake," "committee," or "venue."

- A vulture can fly up to 40 miles per hour.

- The vulture plays an important part in keeping the environment clean by eating dead animals.

WEASEL

MAKING A U-TURN IN A NARROW TUNNEL IS QUITE A TALENT!

Type of animal:
Mammal

Find it in the Bible
Leviticus 11:29 NI

The weasel is a meat-eating mammal with a long, slender body and a tail almost as long as i body. It has a small head with long whiskers. Most species have a dark brown upper coat an a white belly. Some weasels shed their summer coats and grow white ones during the winte Depending on the species, the weasel grows from five to eighteen inches long.

The weasel makes its home in abandoned burrows and under rotting logs, tree roots, or rocks. The nest is made of grass and leaves and is lined with fur.

The weasel is very aggressive when its territory is invaded. Because it has such a slender build, it can chase prey such as mice or voles down their narrow tunnels. Its long, slender body can even make a U-turn in the tunnel if an exit is needed.

The weasel's speed, fierceness, and ability to crawl into tight spaces helps it cope with an array of predators. It also has a reputation for cleverness. The weasel uses its tail to help defend its food and territory against other weasels. Certain species of weasels perform the "weasel war dance" after fighting with other animals. During this "dance," the weasel arches its back and hops sideways and backward as it makes hissing noises.

The weasel was common in the Holy Land, although it is mentioned only once in the Bible. According to Mosaic Law, it is considered an unclean animal. The Hebrew word translated "weasel" probably translates as "mole." Several Bible translations use the word mo instead of "weasel."

DID YOU KNOW. . .

- A weasel can climb trees and is a good swimmer.
- The weasel releases a musk odor when it is frightened.
- A group of weasels is called a "boogle," "gang," "pack," or "confusion."

ype of animal:

lammal

ind it in the Bible:

ienesis 1:21 KJV

WHALE

CAN A WHALE SING?

he whale is the largest animal in the world. Even though it lives in the ocean, it is not a fish. is a mammal because it is warm-blooded, has lungs and breathes air, and has hair on its ody.

When a whale breathes, it raises its head up out of the water high enough to take in air. It reathes in and out through its blowhole, which opens and lets out used air in a cough that ooks like a waterspout. When the whale takes in new air, it shuts its blowhole and slides its ead back under the water. The blue whale's "blow" can reach as high as thirty feet.

When a whale sleeps, it stays at the surface of the water with the blowhole above the irface. Because it must breathe r, it takes short naps instead of eeping for long periods at a time.

The blue whale is the loudest nimal in the world. It moans, roans, squeaks, and talks nderwater where sounds travel reat distances. The humpback vhale has a song that lasts thirty-ve minutes.

Some whales are quite crobatic, making leaps out of he water called "breaching." The vhale swims by moving its tail up nd down and using its flippers to urn. It glides and takes long, deep ives. The sperm whale has been nown to dive to depths of 655 to '80 feet.

There are two types of whales—

A giant blue whale expels moist air from its "blow hole."

those without teeth and those with teeth. The whale with teeth (called a "toothed whale") eats small fish and squid and hunts in groups called "pods." The sperm whale is a toothed whale.

The whale without teeth (called a "baleen whale") swims with its mouth open and takes in water filled with fish, plankton, and plants. It then pushes the water back out while straining out the food through the baleen in its mouth. The blue whale, the largest whale on earth at up to one hundred feet long, is a baleen whale.

A whale cannot see well underwater, especially when the water is dark and murky, so it depends on hearing. Toothed whales make clicking noises that sound like a very fast typewriter or high whistle. When they do that, they wait for an echo of the clicks to bounce off an object and come back to them. This tells the whale how far away an object is. This process is called "echolocation."

Whales are found in every ocean around the world. They migrate farther than any other animal. In warm summer months, they feast to build up blubber and other fat reserves. Then when weather and water cool, they migrate to warmer areas where they can find food. They do not stop to eat. They stop only for short periods to rest.

The first mention of the whale is in Genesis when God created the world and all things in it. The King James Version and The Message specifically refer to whales, but other translations call the animals God created "sea monsters" or "sea creatures."

When you see a whale's tail—also called a "fluke"—above water like this, you can bet the whale is probably beginning a dive deep into the water!

JESUS MENTIONS THE WHALE

The Pharisees and teachers of law came to Jesus one day and said, "Teacher, we want to see a miraculous sign from you."

Jesus answered and said, "Evil and unfaithful people ask for signs. I will not give you one except the sign of the prophet Jonah. Remember, Jonah was in the whale for three days and three nights. Something like this will happen to the Son of Man. He will spend three days and three nights in the grave"

See Matthew 12:38–41

WAS IT REALLY A WHALE THAT SWALLOWED JONAH?

Some Bible scholars do not believe that a whale could have swallowed Jonah. They speak of a big fish or a "sea monster." Perhaps God created a special fish that swallowed Jonah. The sperm whale has a gullet large enough to hold the body of a man. The only other animal capable of swallowing a man would be a large great white shark. The white shark was not uncommon in the Mediterranean Sea area.

DID YOU KNOW. . .

- The whale's flippers are very similar in design to a human hand.

- The grey whale migrates up to fifty-five hundred miles, the longest migration of any mammal on earth.

- When a whale rests, it lies still at the water's surface with its tail hanging down and part of its head near the surface. This is called "logging."

- Some whales can swim at speeds of up to 30 miles per hour.

WILD GOAT

WOW! CAN THAT GOAT JUMP!

Type of animal:
Mammal

Find it in the Bible
Psalm 104:18

The wild goat resembles the common domestic goat, but it is much larger. The wild goat's horns are longer than the domestic goat's, sometimes a yard in length. Its horns are curved and surrounded by many rings and ridges. The wild goat uses its horns for spearing, thrusting, and warding off predators. It also uses its horns to fight off other wild goats during mating season.

In the wild, the female and young wild goats live in flocks of up to five hundred animals. Most grown males are solitary animals except when they are ready to mate.

Wild goats generally live in rugged mountain country. They climb up rough and narrow places and jump from one rock to another. Their small hooves are hollowed underneath and have a sort of ridge around them, which helps the goats cling to the rocks without slipping.

Wild goats migrate to higher ground in the spring and return to the lower ground in winter. They migrate in search of food—grass, twigs, berries, and bark. They are highly dependent on a source of water, because they need to drink every two or three days. If a source of water dries up, wild goats move to another area.

David wrote in the Psalms about the wild goats belonging to the high mountains. According to the Mosaic Law, the wild goat is a clean animal that the Israelites could eat. The wild goat is also called "mountain goat" in some Bible translations.

DID YOU KNOW. . .

- Both male and female wild goats have short beards.
- The life span of a wild goat is twelve to twenty-two years.
- The wild goat has heavy wool that helps it survive the harsh mountain winter climate.

WILD OX

Type of animal:
Mammal

Find it in the Bible:
Psalm 29:6

WHERE IS THE WILD OX TODAY?

The wild ox mentioned in the Bible is a mysterious animal. Different versions of the Bible call it different names—wild ox, unicorn, rhinoceros, or antelope. Job 39:9–12 describes this animal as being so large, powerful, and wild that no one could control it, tame it, or train it.

While it would be hard to know for certain what species of animal it really was, some Bible scholars believe it could be the gigantic aurochs, a huge bovine animal (in the same group of animals as modern-day cattle) that lived during biblical times but is now extinct. The aurochs was much larger than today's cattle, standing as tall as six and a half feet and weighing as much as twenty-two hundred pounds.

The aurochs had long, thick horns that pointed forward rather than sweeping out to the side. Cave paintings from various sites show the male aurochs as being mostly black, while the female and young were red in color.

This animal lived in the forest and open scrubland, but it could be found in grasslands as well. It grazed on grass, leaves, herbs, and fruit.

OTHER BIBLE VERSES THAT MENTION THE "WILD OX" OR "UNICORN" ARE NUMBERS 24:8; DEUTERONOMY 33:17; PSALM 22:21; 92:10; AND ISAIAH 34:7.

Since some Bible translations, including the King James Version, call the wild ox a "unicorn," some Bible scholars believe it was a rhinoceros. The fact that the rhinoceros is also large, strong, and has one large horn makes that a possibility.

The wild ox is mentioned in the Bible in connection with the strength of the nation of Israel (Numbers 24:8) and in connection with the goodness and power of God (Psalm 29:5–6).

DID YOU KNOW . . .

- The original Hebrew word for wild ox, *re'em*, refers to a wild, untamable animal of great strength with a mighty horn or horns.

- The Bible describes the wild ox as a very powerful, aggressive creature.

- The aurochs, which some believe is the wild ox of the Bible, became extinct in the early 1600s.

153

WOLF

HOW CAN A WOLF COMMUNICATE WITHOUT MAKING A SOUND?

Type of animal:
Mammal

Find it in the Bible:
John 10:12

The wolf is the largest member of the canine family of animals, which includes the domestic dog, the fox, the coyote, and other doglike animals. Its long, thick hair is mostly gray or a mixture of black, gray, tan, brown, and white.

The wolf is a fierce and dangerous hunter that usually feeds on small animals but will also attack and kill deer, sheep, and even cattle when it is hungry enough. If it is really hungry, a large adult wolf can eat as much as twenty-two pounds of meat at one time. But when food is scarce, it can go several weeks without eating.

The wolf is an intelligent animal that is loyal to other wolves. Though a few wolves are loners, they usually travel and hunt in packs. The packs usually include seven or eight members, but wolves have been known to run with packs of up to twenty animals. The wolf pack hunts over and over in the same territorial hunting routes.

Sometimes the wolf howls, but it can also bark, whine, yelp, and snarl like a domestic dog. A wolf can also communicate with another wolf without making a sound. When the wolf's ears point straight up and its teeth are bared, it is giving a warning. When it narrows its eyes and flattens its ears against its head, it is saying, "What's going on here?" When the wolf holds its tail high, it communicates the message, "I'm in charge!" When a wolf tucks its tail between its legs, it is saying, "I won't argue." When the wolf is happy, it tilts its head and wiggles its body from side to side.

The wolf has a keen sense of hearing and can detect sounds from up to six miles away. Touch and smell are important as it sniffs out prey. It has good eyesight to catch nearby movements.

The female wolf gives birth to litters of five or six babies in a den that is underground or dug into the side of a sandy hill. The baby wolves, which weigh about one pound at birth, are called "pups."

A wolf pack takes some time to rest before heading out to hunt.

The wolf was common in Palestine in biblical times. It was a constant threat to flocks of sheep and earned a reputation of being vicious as it stalked prey at night.

Wolves are mentioned in the Bible several times. Sometimes the Bible uses the word wolf to refer to cruel and evil leaders. The prophet Isaiah foretold the peaceful reign when Jesus returns to earth as a time when "the wolf will live with the lamb" (11:6 NIV). Jesus also spoke of those who opposed His message as "wolves."

JESUS' WARNING: YOU WILL ENCOUNTER THE WOLVES!

Jesus called His twelve disciples and gave them instructions about going out to teach and to heal the sick. He told them to heal the sick, raise the dead, heal people with leprosy, and drive out demons (see Matthew 10:8).

He instructed His followers to take no clothes or money with them but to rely on others to provide for them. Then Jesus said, "I am sending you out like sheep among wolves" (Matthew 10:16 NIV). Jesus warned His disciples so that they would be on their guard against people who would try to mistreat them because they preached the gospel message.

OTHER BIBLE VERSES THAT MENTION WOLVES ARE GENESIS 49:27; ISAIAH 65:25; JEREMIAH 5:6; EZEKIEL 22:27; HABAKKUK 1:8; ZEPHANIAH 3:3; MATTHEW 7:15; AND ACTS 20:29.

DID YOU KNOW. . .

- A wolf can run in short bursts at up to 38 miles per hour for hours without tiring.

- The wolf is known for howling, which it does mostly at night.

- A full-grown wolf can leap as high as a one-story building!

- Wolves are usually more frightened of humans than humans are of them.

WORM

WHY SO MANY WORMS ON THE GROUND AFTER A RAIN?

Type of animal:
Annelid (earthworm or insect (larva)

Find it in the Bible
Deuteronomy 28:3

The worm is a soft-bodied animal without a backbone, arms, or legs. Some worms cannot move on their own but must wait on natural forces or animals to move them. Others have bristles or fins that help them move.

Worms are divided into three groups—flatworms, roundworms, and segmented worms. The flatworm has a flat, ribbon-shaped body with a pair of eyes at the front. The roundworm is found in damp soil and moss but can also live in water. The segmented worm has a body divided into segments or rings.

The best-known worms are the earthworms, which are from a group of animals called "annelids." They are valuable to gardens and farmer's crops. They tunnel deeply in soil, secreting slime that contains nitrogen, which helps plants grow.

Most worms need to live in moist places. If a worm's skin dries out, it will die.

Many worms do not die if they lose a body part. They can replace or repair any body segment but the head.

There are many Bible passages where insect larvae are called "worms." Larvae of insects, such as the moth, eat clothing made from wool. Some kinds of worms are destructive to grapevines and other crops.

The Bible also uses the worm as a symbol of lowliness or weakness (Psalm 22:6). In other verses, the worm is alive and working in a place for the unbeliever and wicked (see Mark 9:48).

DID YOU KNOW...

- Many earthworms are found above ground after a heavy rainfall because they can drown underground.

- In one acre of land, there can be more than a billion earthworms.

- Worms come in every size, from microscopic worms to the African giant earthworm, which can grow up to twenty-two feet long.

SCRIPTURE INDEX

SCRIPTURE INDEX

ART CREDITS

About Jane Landreth

Jane Landreth enjoys touching young lives with God's love. She taught school until her son, Eric, was born, then officially launched her writing career, using her son's adventures for her first story and article ideas. Later other ideas came from teaching children in church. She and her husband, Jack, reside in the Ozarks, where she continues writing for children and teaches writing in conferences and school classrooms. This is her third book for Barbour, having previously written *Bible Prayers for Bedtime* and *Bible Miracles for Bedtime*.